WATCH
YOUR WALK

RICHARD BAXTER

WATCH YOUR WALK

MINISTERING FROM A HEART OF INTEGRITY

INTRODUCTION BY

DR. RICHARD C. HALVERSON

EDITED BY

JAMES M. HOUSTON

Victor®

The Bible Teacher's Teacher

COOK COMMUNICATIONS MINISTRIES
Colorado Springs, Colorado • Paris, Ontario
KINGSWAY COMMUNICATIONS LTD
Eastbourne, England

Victor® is an imprint of
Cook Communications Ministries, Colorado Springs, CO 80918
Cook Communications, Paris, Ontario
Kingsway Communications, Eastbourne, England

WATCH YOUR WALK
This abridged edition

Unless otherwise noted, all Scripture quotations are Richard Baxter's par-
aphrase of the King James version of the Bible. Italics used in Scripture
are for emphasis.

Cover Design by: Jackson Design CO, LLC/Greg Jackson.

First Printing, 2005
Printed in United States of America
1 2 3 4 5 6 7 8 9 10 Printing/Year 08 07 06 05

First published 1982 by Multnomah Press, Portland, Oregon 97266 U.S.A.

Library of Congress Cataloging-in-Publication Data

Baxter, Richard, 1615-1691.
  [Gildas Salvianus]
  Watch your walk : a pattern for personal growth and ministry / Richard
Baxter ; abridged and edited by James M. Houston ; introduction by
Richard C. Halverson.
      p. cm. -- (Victor classics)
  Originally published: The reformed pastor. Portland, Or. : Multnomah
Press, c1982.
  Includes bibliographical references and indexes.
  ISBN 0-7814-4179-X (pbk. : alk. paper)
  1. Clergy--Office--Early works to 1800. 2. Pastoral theology--Early works
to 1800. I. Houston, J. M. (James Macintosh), 1922- II. Title. III. Series.
  BV659.B39 2005
  253--dc22
                          2004025505

Dr. James M. Houston was born to missionary parents who served in Spain. Dr. Houston served as University Lecturer at Oxford University, England, from 1949 to 1971. He was a Fellow of Hertford College during the period between 1964 and 1971, and held the office of Principal of Regent College from 1969 to 1978. He has served as Chancellor of Regent College and is currently Emeritus Professor of Spiritual Theology.

Dr. Houston has been active in the establishment and encouragement of lay training centers across the continents. These include the C. S. Lewis Institute in Washington, D.C., and the London Institute for the Study of Contemporary Christianity. In addition to his work with the classics series, he has published a book titled I Believe in the Creator *(Eerdmans, 1978).*

CONTENTS

PREFACE TO
VICTOR CLASSICS

With the profusion of books now being published, most Christian readers require some guidance for a basic collection of spiritual works that will remain lifelong companions. This new series of Christian classics of devotion is being edited to provide just such a basic library for the home. Those selected may not all be commonly known today, but each has a central concern of relevance for the contemporary Christian.

Another goal for this collection of books is a reawakening. It is a reawakening to the spiritual thoughts and meditations of the forgotten centuries. Many Christians today have no sense of the past. If the Reformation is important to them, they jump from the apostolic church to the sixteenth century, forgetting some fourteen centuries of the work of the Holy Spirit among many devoted to Christ. These classics will remove that gap and enrich their readers by the faith and devotion of God's saints through all history.

And so we turn to the books and to their purpose. Some books have changed the lives of their readers. Notice how Athanasius's *Life of Antony* affected Augustine or William Law's *A Serious Call to a Holy Life* influenced John Wesley. Others, such as Augustine's *Confessions* or Thomas à Kempis's

Imitation of Christ, have remained perennial sources of inspiration throughout the ages. We sincerely hope those selected in this series will have a like effect on our readers.

Each one of the classics chosen for this series is deeply significant to a contemporary Christian leader. In some cases, the thoughts and reflections of the classic writer are mirrored in the leader's genuine ambitions and desires today, an unusual pairing of hearts and minds across the centuries. And thus these individuals have been asked to write the introduction on the book that has been so meaningful to his or her own life.

EDITING THE CLASSICS

Such classics of spiritual life have had their obstacles. Their original language, the archaic style of later editions, their length, the digressions, the allusions to bygone cultures—all make the use of them discouraging to the modern reader. To reprint them (as was done on a massive scale in the last century and still so today) does not overcome these handicaps of style, length, and language. To seek the kernel and remove the husk, this series involves therefore the abridging, rewriting, and editing of each book. At the same time we sought to keep to the essential message given in the work and to pursue as much as possible the author's original style.

The principles of editing are as follows. Keep sentences short. Paragraphs are also shortened. Material is abridged where there are digressions or allusions made that are time binding. Archaic words are altered. Spelling is that of *Webster's Dictionary, 11th edition*. Logical linkage may have to be added to abridged material. The identity of theme or argument is kept sharply in mind. Allusions to other authors are given brief explanation.

For the Christian, the Bible is the basic text for spiritual reading. All other devotional reading is secondary and should never be a substitute for it. Therefore, the allusions to Scripture in these classics of devotion are searched out and referenced in the text. This is where other editions of these books may ignore the scriptural quality of these works, which are inspired and guided by the Bible. The biblical focus is always the hallmark of truly Christian spirituality.

PURPOSE FOR THE CLASSICS: SPIRITUAL READING

Since our sensate and impatient culture makes spiritual reading strange and difficult for us, the reader should be cautioned to read these books slowly, meditatively, and reflectively. One cannot rush through them like a detective story. In place of novelty, they focus on remembrance, reminding us of values that remain of eternal consequence. We may enjoy many new things, but values are as old as God's creation.

The goal for the reader of these books is not to seek information. Instead, these volumes teach one about living wisely. That takes obedience; submission of will; change of heart; and a tender, docile spirit. When John the Baptist saw Jesus, he reacted, "He must increase, and I must decrease." Likewise, spiritual reading decreases our natural instincts, to allow His love to increase within us.

Nor are these books "how-to" kits or texts. They take us as we are—that is, as persons, and not as functionaries. They guide us to "be" authentic and not necessarily to help us to promote more professional activities. Such books require us to make time for their slow digestion, space to let their thoughts enter into our hearts, and discipline to let new insights "stick" and become part of our Christian character.

James M. Houston

EDITOR'S NOTE ABOUT BAXTER AND THE RELEVANCE OF THIS CLASSIC

THE MAN

Constant ill health characterized the long and hectic life of Richard Baxter (1615–1691). Even so he produced enough material (mostly in the areas of practical divinity and pastoral theology) to fill twenty-three volumes in the nineteenth-century edition of his work by William Orme (1830).

Baxter lived through a period of England's history that was both disruptive and creative. His life somewhat pictured the tumultuous collision of these forces. Although ordained an Episcopalian, he sorrowfully rejected the stance the Episcopal church took at the Restoration, that "Episcopal ordination is essential for the practice of Christian ministry." Consequently, along with some 1,800 dissenters, he became a nonconformist and was expelled from his ministry at Kidderminster, where he had labored fourteen years.

Baxter retired to London to preach, where he also suffered twenty-one months' imprisonment at the age of seventy. He died five years later. Some 135 items he penned were published during his life, and 5 posthumous works were later printed.

As a statesman, Baxter was a failure. He refused a bishopric when it was offered to him. And though he was the nonconformists' chief spokesman for twenty years, he was too outspoken to lead them politically. While his heart desired peace to heal schism, he was always too blunt and plainspoken to build bridges.

But as a pastor, Richard Baxter was incomparable. And it is this ability that is expressed in this, his best-known work. His record at Kidderminster is perhaps one of the greatest in pastoral achievement in the history of the church. He taught his congregation individually through pastoral counseling, and systematically he catechized (i.e., taught, by method of question and answer) them in basic Christianity. What Baxter teaches and expresses in *Watch Your Walk* (originally, *Gilda Salvianus*, later retitled *The Reformed Pastor*, 1656) he actually put into practice in his own ministry. That is why this book is so burning in its conviction, so practical and lifelike in its application, and so honest and candid in its understanding of human needs.

HIS WRITING

The best term to describe Baxter's style is *wordy*. He found it difficult to stop writing. He can be repetitive, long-winded, and virtually encyclopedic in his advice. Editors have therefore found the need to reduce the bulkiness of his works. Even his defense against objections to the first edition of *Watch Your Walk* runs into thirty-nine pages. (He made it into an appendix for later editions.)

The looseness of his style to a certain degree is compensated for by the detailed points he emphasizes as a spiritual director. He does direct specifically and clearly. For someone writing in the seventeenth century to a Puritan audience, he gathered from a wide variety of sources. He is evidently well versed in his contemporaries. But it is impressive how much he also knows and refers to the great Christian fathers such as Bernard of Clairvaux, Augustine, Gregory, and Cyprian, as well as to later church writers.

Controversy and schism marked his age. Baxter tried to avoid it but did not always succeed. Editing, therefore, reduces both his wordiness (approximately 580 pages) and many specific allusions to theological debate that are irrelevant for the modern reader. That which remains in this edition we trust is the vitality and conviction of the man, his sincerity and honesty, and the relational and realistic ways in which he gives counsel.

His forthrightness shows itself in the original title of the book. *Gilda Salvianus* refers to two writers of the fifth and sixth centuries, who were blunt in castigating the sins of their generations. "By their names," he said, "I offer you an excuse ... for plain dealing."

The Reformed Pastor was the subtitle. By "Reformed," Baxter did not mean Protestant or even Calvinist; he meant a revitalized pastor, renewed in heart and spirit to serve God fully. The ministry of England in the seventeenth century sadly needed such renewal. His book now helps to focus our attention on today and on our need for renewal. One of the major criticisms that Baxter made was about the lack of church discipline, which is missing in the life of the contemporary church. Finally, he saw the importance of personal counseling, which, in this modern age of mass-minded, church-growth technocracy, also needs a renewed emphasis.

And for the layman, Baxter writes about the serious need for informed instruction. He also strongly advocates the delegation of duties according to gifts in the congregation so that all might use their gifts for God. These teachings are needed greatly today.

THE BOOK

Indeed, the influence of *Watch Your Walk* has been both lasting and powerful in the church's life since Baxter's day. Unlike some of the lesser-known works in the Victor Classics, *Watch Your Walk* is a book celebrated for its perennial popularity. In the edition edited by J. T. Wilkinson, one can read about the influence of this work during the past 300 years.

Philip Jacob Spener, the founder of German pietism, was influenced by Baxter's book as a student at Strasbourg. The book was translated into German in 1716.[1] Cotton Mather, the historian of New England churches, affirmed its influence there.[2]

Philip Doddridge thought the book "a most extraordinary performance and should be read by every young minister, before he takes a people under his stated 'care.'" He thought the practical instructions of the book should be reread every three or four years.[3] Charles Spurgeon thought "Richard Baxter is the most forceful of writers, and if you want to know the art of pleading read ... his *[Watch Your Walk]*."[4] In the 1821 edition, William Brown urged "the different Missionary Societies ... to furnish every missionary, or at least every Missionary Station, with a copy of *[Watch Your Walk]*."

Today there are many manuals available on leadership techniques. Just this one slim volume might help to counterbalance the managerial emphasis that authors urge for contemporary church life. For there is also the need to have a pastor's heart in the work of the Lord.

One further word is necessary about the writing found in *Watch Your Walk*. Richard Baxter had a personal idiosyncrasy that has been corrected in this edition of the book. At times, he lists or outlines what he is going to deal with and then, when he begins writing, is inconsistent with that order. Therefore, to be consistent with the plan outlined at the end of the first chapter, we have arranged his sequence so that chapter 1 is followed by chapters 4, 2, 5, 3, 6, 7, 8, and 9 of his original edition. The insertion of part divisions into the table of contents and the text material itself is meant also as an aid to clarity.

Few among us today more exemplify *watching one's walk* than Dr. Richard Halverson. His own pastoral ministry at Hollywood Presbyterian Church in Los Angeles and then at Fourth Presbyterian Church in Washington, D.C., has had national significance. This is further heightened by his ministry as chaplain to the United States Senate.

The warm personal concern that Dr. Halverson has long exemplified in church life, and in his lifelong ministry with the Fellowship movement, makes him a pastor's pastor. We are richly indebted to him for endorsing a book he largely illustrates by his own example. Its principles, which he upholds and recommends, are vitally needed for the future well-being of the church universal.

James M. Houston

NOTES

[1] Richard Baxter, *The Reformed Pastor*, John T. Wilkinson, ed. (London: Epworth Press, 1939), p. 32.

[2] Ibid., p. 33.

[3] Ibid., p. 36.

[4] Ibid., p. 45.

INTRODUCTION

There are a number of reasons why Richard Baxter's book *Watch Your Walk* is relevant for churches and their pastors at this particular time. In the first place, it reveals the truth about the Puritans, as to their lifestyle and beliefs. This description contrasts with the negative image that is commonly held and that has brought the authentic puritan spirit into disrepute.

The stereotype of the Puritans is that they were narrow, legalistic, inflexible, exclusive, bigoted, and pietistic in the ugliest ways. Page after page, paragraph after paragraph, sentence after sentence, Baxter's instruction exposes that stereotype as a crude caricature and commends the authentic puritan ethos to the most critical observer.

Second, the book encourages those who are discouraged about the church. Each generation tends to consider its own bad characteristics as the worst ills history has ever known. In a similar manner the church has its many detractors today, within as well as without. Their pessimism often makes one feel that the church has never been as corrupt and impotent as it is at the present time. Yet one of the most beneficial results of a knowledge of history is to put current events into perspective. Baxter's insights into the church of his day encourage the reader to hope in the renewing power of the Holy Spirit.

Jesus Christ meant it when He said, "I will build my Church;

and the gates of hell shall not prevail against it" (Matt. 16:18). In its humanness the church fails often and in many ways. Baxter's day was one of almost unbelievable deviation. Nevertheless, Christ kept His Word, and His church was preserved through that time, just as she will be in our day and to the moment of His consummate triumph in history.

There is much to be discouraged about in the church today, but there is much about which to be greatly encouraged. Consider what Jesus began in an intimate relationship with twelve men in a three-year period: it has continued for 2,000 years. It has reached and transformed the lives of millions and millions, transcending all barriers that divide humans. Today it continues stronger than ever. Such success literally forces one to believe in the church that Jesus said would be indestructible. Empires rise and fall, kingdoms come and go, but the church of Christ perseveres. Baxter lived in a day when it would have been easy to give up on the church. Yet he believed in it and lived, worked, and died for it.

A third reason for the book's relevance is that we live at a time when "church growth" has become virtually a science. Growth is thought of primarily quantitatively—in terms of numbers, rather than qualitatively—in terms of spiritual nurture and edification. Baxter's emphasis on the careful nurture of each member will constitute an inspiring alternative to the "big business" success syndrome.

When I was called to the Fourth Presbyterian Church in 1958, I had an agreement with the officers that there would be no pressure to increase the membership. It was understood that our responsibility was to care for the people, nurture them in the Word of God, strengthen their fellowship with Christ and one another, and help them grow in love. The conviction was that numerical growth, as it occurred in the New Testament, was the spontaneous and normal result of a healthy community of faith (Acts 2:47; 6:7; 9:31; 16:5).

Through the years there were complaints from some non-members who attended; they wondered if we were indifferent toward folks uniting with the church. We were not, but the emphasis was so centered on the care and nurture of the faithful that we simply made no effort to recruit and receive members. Little by little, methods were developed that were designed to make uniting with the church as meaningful as possible and to help those who joined know clearly what they were doing. In twenty-two years the membership nearly quadrupled, and many came to Christ who remained in their own churches. This was especially true of youth.

This did not mean an indifference to evangelism on the part of our church. From my birth in Christ, I was discipled in the Pauline principle that a believer is a debtor to the whole world to reach it for Christ. No joy can compare with that of seeing a soul pass from death to life, and one would like to see every person born of God. But it was, and still is, our conviction that the New Testament does not define evangelism as a department of church life. Nor is it one of many programs initiated by the church. Rather, it is the normal outcome of a spiritually strong community, the quality of whose life, individually and corporately, supports the witness of the believers.

The love of God is characterized by a longing for the eternal welfare of every living soul. The surest way for this to be manifested is through faithful instruction in the whole counsel of God for every believer. This was fundamental to Baxter's understanding of the pastor. "The *first* and main point I submit to you is that it is an unquestionable duty of all ministers of the church to catechize and to teach personally all who are submitted to their care" (chap. 1, p. 33).

A fourth reason Baxter's discussions are so valuable today is his concern for the family, a concern that became a care in his pastoral shepherding of the family and each of its members in the context of the whole body. We should welcome his example to the twenty-first-century church when love, marriage, the family, and the home seem under such intense attack.

It is indisputable that a culture cannot endure indefinitely the disintegration of marriage, the family, and the home. The family is central to the perpetuation and preservation of humanity, basic to social order, and the primary environment for instruction and growth. God's command to Israel included the responsibility of religious instruction in the family (Deut. 6:4–9). In the family, value systems are established; authority, discipline, love, respect are learned; life's direction is set. Though a child in later years may seem largely to repudiate what was learned in the home, he certainly has a great advantage over the one who did not enjoy a family orientation in faith. In crisis he will generally return to his roots.

> "Let the children hear the mighty deed
>   which God performed of old;
> Which in our younger years we saw,
>   And which our fathers told.
>
> "He bids us make his glories known,
>   His works of power and grace;
> And we'll convey his wonders down
>   Through every rising race.
>
> "Our lips shall tell them to our sons,
>   And they again to theirs,

That generations yet unborn

May teach them to their heirs."

[Ps. 78—Metered Psalms adapted to social, private, and public worship. Presbyterian Church, USA—1843.]

Richard Baxter centers his instruction in the family. He writes: "We spend Mondays and Tuesdays from morning to about nightfall, taking some fifteen or sixteen families each week in this work of catechism. With two assistants we make our way through all of the congregation—eight hundred families—and teach each family during the year." Baxter kept "notes of what each family member has learned, so [he] could continue" instruction systematically (Chap. 1 pp. 34–35).

A fifth reason *Watch Your Walk* merits reading today is central to its message: Baxter's instruction turns again and again to the pastor himself. He is never very far from insightful, loving (but not always gentle) reproof and correction of the pastor's effectiveness with the people to whom God has given him charge. Yet he always writes about this with a positive, encouraging rationale. All of us as pastors need to "take heed" to ourselves as Paul advised the elders of Ephesus (Acts 20:28) and as Baxter advocates. Certainly the church will not rise above its leadership. The pastor's personal and family life must come under the scrutiny of Scripture continually. In the light of Holy Writ, the one called to such high vocation must aspire to holiness and purity of life.

Throughout my pastorates, I have found a daily time of private nurture and prayer to be absolutely essential to my effectiveness. By the time I had graduated from seminary, I had gone through the legalistic phase during which I spent time daily in personal devotions for its own sake. This included many "guilt trips" when I failed. Early in the pastorate I discovered the necessity of personal devotions for the sake of my own spiritual nurture and for guarding my relationship to Christ.

The pastor's life under Scripture's scrutiny is a principle from Baxter that is not always easy to apply. One lesson that came with difficulty and relatively late for me was my responsibility to my wife and children. Early in the ministry I justified neglect of them on the grounds of responsibilities to the church. I had to learn that Christ expected me to love my wife as He loved His church and to care for my children. Though the tension is rarely absent, the work must never be allowed to come before one's relationship to Christ or spouse and family.

Baxter's chapter on "The Pastor's Need of Repentance" is strangely contemporary. He discusses responsibility to the poor and the sins of neglecting those for whom God is a constant advocate. In a number of unexpected contexts, Baxter reminds us of the obligation implicit in our calling: be sensitive, compassionate, and responsive toward the unfortunate.

Concern over biblical illiteracy today is the sixth reason for this classic's relevancy. Even in evangelical churches the sparsity of biblical exposition from the pulpit is a matter for serious consideration. The result is that it is not uncommon for the church as an institution, and its members in particular, to confront contemporary social problems from a sociological, psychological, or political point of view. The absolute, unbending moral truths of the Scriptures are less and less used as criteria for resolving ethical and social issues. In the words of Harry Blamires, "There is no Christian mind." Baxter's emphasis and insistence on biblical instruction could not be more timely and relevant in such a day.

Dr. Luke was inspired by the Holy Spirit to record the fact that the apostolic church, fresh from the Pentecostal event, devoted itself to four things (Acts 2:42): "apostolic teaching and fellowship, breaking of bread and prayer." Apostolic doctrine was essential to the New Testament community and is indispensable to the health and strength of the community of faith today. There was a reawakening to the need for the Bible centuries later in the church. In the Reformation, the pulpit with the open Bible replaced the altar. Our Lord's sacrifice became no less important; it was still to be remembered regularly in the celebration of Communion. But the emphasis emerged that the people of God needed to be taught doctrine.

The pulpit is dedicated to the exposition of the Word of God, and there is no greater need in the church today. I shall never cease to be grateful for the homiletics teacher in seminary, Dr. Andrew W. Blackwood, who schooled his students in biblical preaching. His course "Planning a Year's Sermons" turned out to be one of the most valuable for me. From my first pastorate through the last, I followed this plan with great satisfaction. Not only did it expedite and enhance sermon preparation, but it meant following the events of the church year and, in general, covering all parts of the Bible annually.

The seventh reason for this book's relevance centers on the word *disciple*. If he were living today, Baxter would be a strong advocate of what is now called "discipleship." Though a good biblical word, it is of rather recent discovery and general use. It is hoped this good word and its practice will not be a temporary fad that is merely a redundant slogan due to overuse.

Baxter emphasized the pastor's responsibility to know the needs of the people in his parish and to feed them individually. His practice of spending time for instruction with each member of his good-sized congregation ought to rebuke and inspire every pastor who reads about it.

His insistence on such precise care and oversight of the community of Christ is fundamental to pastoral work. In Baxter's own words, "As a careful shepherd looks after all sheep, or as a good schoolmaster looks after every individual student, or as a good doctor who knows each of his patients" (chap. 5, p. 110). His purpose (chap. 5, pp. 106–107) for pastoral ministry is essential. His classification of the members and their needs is brilliant (chap. 5, pp. 110–116).

At some time during the second year of my first pastorate, I was captivated by a text in Mark's gospel (3:14) where it is recorded, "Jesus chose twelve and ordained them to be with him." The importance of this simple text to my future ministry was absolutely incalculable. Jesus was going to start a movement that would reach the whole world and last forever. He had three years in which to do it. And He deliberately devoted Himself to twelve men. He did not neglect the multitudes, but He "discipled" twelve men. It occurred to me that such a strategy could not be improved upon, and it gave me direction for my ministry to the present moment.

Interestingly, for years it has been my observation that the imperative that evangelicals have communicated from the Great Commission (Matt. 28:18–20) has been to go. *Go!* has been the big word, and tremendous pressure has been exerted, especially on youthful audiences, to *go!* Generally that meant overseas. As a matter of fact, the word *go* is a participle, and the only command in the Great Commission is "make disciples."

Whatever else Baxter did as a pastor, he discipled the people. At a time when the condition of the church was deplorably corrupt, Baxter unswervingly discipled the flock. And he speaks to us today with great relevance and urgency.

Finally, Baxter's passion for unity is yet another compelling reason to read *Watch Your Walk*. One gathers from his writing that it was virtually a preoccupation with him. He moved in a direction contrary to that of the puritan stereotype, with its legalistic, separatistic, narrow exclusiveness. Instead Baxter earnestly exhorts pastors concerning their need of each other and the fundamental oneness of the body of Christ.

Reflecting on *Watch Your Walk*, one has the sense of actually completing a seminary course on pastoral ministerial practice—in the most meticulous, specific, and explicit detail. As I read and pondered, I wished I had taken such a course in seminary with which to begin my ministry. Baxter's instruction contains precepts and principles that I learned relatively late in my pastorates.

Perhaps, however, I would not have appreciated *Watch Your Walk* as a student. I might have relegated it to the realm of theory. Perhaps it is a work appreciated only by those initiated into ministry, for that is when one is involved in pastoral work and begins to learn the relevance and/or irrelevance of a seminary education to the actual.

In any event, this book comes to us out of the past, from one who took pastoring seriously. It is a welcome, wholesome prescription for the contemporary church.

Dr. Richard C. Halverson
Former Chaplain, United States Senate

CHAPTER 1

AN INTRODUCTION FOR PASTORS AND LAYMEN

Let me tell you the background to this work. The Lord awakened His servants in this country and in some neighborly districts to a sense of their duty in teaching the faith. After they had proposed to accomplish this goal by catechism (i.e., close questioning about the principles of religion) and private instruction of all in their parishes, they made an agreement together. The agreement was that each would catechize his congregation in the future with a deep sense of humility before God and with an attitude of repentance about having neglected for so long to do so.

These servants met together at Worcester, December 4, 1655, to pray earnestly for three requests: pardon of their previous neglect, God's special help in the work they now committed themselves to undertake, and the success of their renewed teaching with their church members. It was for this solemn occasion that I prepared this work, since I was unable to attend personally due to ill health.

TO THE PASTOR

You may object that I should not speak so plainly and sharply against the sins of those in the ministry. Some say that I should not have published this before the whole world.

I confess that I thought there was some validity to this objection. I did so, however, because if we were to be humbled, we must make a plain confession of our sins. We were also confessing *our own sins* and so taking the shame to our own selves. It could be argued we should have translated it into Latin for our professional usage, but when the sin of neglect is open to the world, it is vain to attempt it. All such attempts would only aggravate and increase our shame.

When the sin is in public, the confession should also be in public—if we seek a full remission. Unpardoned sin will never let us rest and prosper. "He that covereth his sins shall not prosper: But whoso confesseth and forsaketh them shall have mercy" (Prov. 28:13).

Too many who engage in the sacred work of the ministry do so obstinately, characterized by self-seeking, negligence, pride, division, and other sins. We must admonish them. If we could see that such would reform without reproof, we would gladly refrain from publishing their faults. But what else can we do? To give up our brethren is incurable; it is wrong. And to bear the vices of the ministers is to promote the ruin of the church.

Imagine that thousands of you are in a leaky ship. Those who should be pumping out the water and stopping the leaks are disporting themselves or asleep. Now, would you not awaken them to their work and call on them to labor for their very lives? Would men think you wrong then if you spoke sharply and urgently to the slothful? Would you not say, "The work must be done, or else we shall be dead men"? Is the ship ready to sink, and you talk of reputation? This is our case, brethren! The work of God must be done!

But there are always some ready to judge others and to pass the blame to them. What I have spoken here, I have tried to do as impartially as I could, and not be partisan. It is likely that some will be offended by me. They may be offended if the reason is the need for church discipline, but not, I hope, because they belong to other denominations.

The thing I desire is that we may all consider how far we may hold communion together. When we cannot do so, at least let us consult and agree together what may be the rules for the management of our differences. Those who make unnecessary divisions among the churches are those, urges the apostle, whom we should mark and avoid (Rom. 16:17). These he calls carnal (1 Cor. 3:1–3).

The *first* and main point I submit to you is that it is the unquestionable duty of all ministers of the church to catechize and to teach personally all who are submitted to their care. This means six things.

- People must be taught the principles of religion and matters essential to salvation.
- They must be taught these principles in the most edifying and beneficial way possible.
- Personal tutorials, examinations, and instruction have many advantages for this learning process.
- Personal instruction is recommended to us by Scripture and by the servants of Christ throughout all ages.
- Since our care and love of our people must extend to

all, we need to catechize and teach all in our congregation.

⊕ Such work should properly take up a considerable part of our time.

Thus I beseech all faithful ministers of Christ that they immediately and effectually carry out such a ministry. For I confess I find from experience such work will effect reform and revival of the faith by the grace of God.

I wonder at myself. Why was I so long held back from doing so obvious and vital a duty? But this happened to me in the way it happens to others, I suppose. I was long convinced of its value, but I was apprehensive of its difficulties. I did not see clearly enough how important it really was. I imagined that people would scorn being involved in it and that very few would want it. Moreover, I did not think I was capable of doing it, having so many other burdens upon me.

Thus I procrastinated for a long time, for which I now ask God's forgiveness. When I did try out personal catechizing and teaching those in my care, I found the difficulties scarcely existed about which I had thought—other than my bodily conditions of ill health. Instead, I found the benefits and comfort of the work to be such that I would not now forgo doing it for all the riches in the world.

I do not presume to prescribe rules or forms for you or to encourage the use of the same catechism or exhortations we use. But let me tell you what I do in my parish. We spend Mondays and Tuesdays from morning to about nightfall taking some fifteen or sixteen families each week in this work of catechism. With two assistants, we make our way through all of the congregation—about 800 families—and teach each family during the year. I have not been refused by a single family when I have asked it to come and visit me. And I find more outward signs of success with those who come than in all my public preaching.

I am forced by the numbers to take a whole family at once, for an hour each. The clerk of the church goes ahead a week beforehand to arrange the schedules of the timetable. I also keep notes of what each family member has learned, so I can continue to systematically teach him or her.

Fellow servants, you have put your hand to the plow of God. You are doubly sanctified and devoted to Him, as Christians and as pastors. Dare you then draw back and refuse to do His work? You see the work of reformation is at a standstill. Yet many obligations compel you to promote it. Dare you now neglect those means by which it should be done? Will you show your faces in a Christian congregation, as ministers of the Gospel, and pray for a revival, when you refuse to use the means by which it may be done? I earnestly beseech you all in the name of God, and for the sake of your people's souls, that you do not do your ministry carelessly and superficially. Do it vigorously and with all your might. Make it your great and serious business to teach the fundamentals of the faith to all the members of your congregation by these private tutorials.

For I perceive that the life of work under God lies in the prudent, effectual ministry of searching men's hearts and setting there the saving truths of faith. I fear most those ministers who preach well and who are unsuited to the private nurture of their members. Yet if we ministers do not devote ourselves to such private ministry, it must be left undone. Let us then be up and doing with all our might the task entrusted to us, and the Lord will be with us.

My second request to the ministers of the church is that they set themselves, without delay, and unanimously so, to practice Christian discipline. For it is a sad situation that so great a duty is so often neglected.

The common cry is that "our congregations are not ready for it. They will not bear it." If, however, you say our churches are incapable of the order and government of Christ, are you not abdicating your responsibility? Do you not encourage men to look out for better societies where that discipline might be had?

I beseech you, therefore, to be ready to give an account to the Chief Shepherd. Be not found unfaithful in the house of God. Do not shrink from the duty because of the trouble it may cause the flesh. (That is such an obvious sign of hypocrisy.) The costliest duties are usually the most important.

My third and last request is that all the faithful ministers of Christ would, without any more delay, unite and associate for the furtherance of this work of the Lord. Thereby they would maintain unity in concord among the various churches. Would that they did not neglect their brotherly meetings for these purposes.

Let none draw back that agreement in the substantials of faith and godliness. If they be indeed Christians, let them be willing to hold communion with each other to the extent that they can. Let them consult how to manage their differences in the way that will least harm the common truths and Christian cause that they all profess to own and withhold.

To the Lay Reader

[At this point, Baxter explains why he has called this work the first part of a book.] I intend, if God enables me and gives me time, to write a second part containing the duty of the people in relation to their pastors. [In this, Baxter hoped to mark out four areas of the pastoral ministry that apply especially to the layperson, informing and exhorting him about the right and necessity of such work]:

- The right and necessity of a pastoral ministry
- The way to know the true church and its ministry from the false teachers
- How far the laity should assist the pastors in the Gospel
- How far the people should submit to their pastors and what other duties they have in such a relationship

But because my time and strength are so uncertain, and I do not know whether I shall ever live to publish this, I dare not let this immediate opportunity slip by me to address the laity.

The caution that I must give you is in three points. The first is the concern that you do not entertain any negative thoughts of your pastors due to our open confession of personal sins. We have exaggerated them that we might be humbled and then reformed.

You know that they are men and not angels whom God has put in offices as church guides. You know that we are imperfect men. Let others pretend they can attain to a sinless perfection. We dare not do it but confess we are sinners. If it would make a man perfect to say he is perfect, or to deliver a man from sin to say, "I have no sins," then this would be a very easy way to perfection.

But for our part, we believe that "if we say that we have no sin, we deceive ourselves, and the truth is not in us" (1 John 1:8). "And that in many things we offend all" (James 3:2). See therefore that you love and imitate the holiness of your pastors, but do not look for opportunities to slight them or disgrace them for their weaknesses.

Second, I want to warn you, as a watchman of your souls, about how some would beguile you. Their main design is to unsettle you and make you believe that you have been all this while misled. With this in mind, they next want to make you suspect your teachers, to contend with them, and finally to reject them. As one of their own has said, "Not one in ten people ground their faith in the Scriptures; rather, they base their understanding on the credit of their teachers." Therefore, they think that if they can bring you to suspect your teachers and reject them, then you will be like sheep without a shepherd.

Finally, their next design is to diminish the authority and sufficiency of Scripture. But they dare not speak out against the Bible, because they have nothing to set up in its place. So instead some of them will tell you of new prophets and revelations, or some of them will tell you they are at a loss to know what to believe themselves, having no religion and certainly not being Christian.

So I warn you: As you love your souls, keep close to Scripture and to the faithful ministry of the Word. Do not despise your shepherds if you wish to escape the wolves. If any question our callings, send them to our writings where we have fully proved ourselves, or send them to us. For, brethren, let me freely speak with you! The ungrateful contempt of a faithful ministry is the shame of this land!

My last advice to you is this: See that you obey your faithful teachers. Take heed that you refuse not to learn what they would teach you. Go to them when they desire to help you. Be thankful for their help. At other times when you need their advice, go to them of your own accord. Ask for it. Their purpose is to be your guide in the way of life. Do not be so proud as to think you are your own spiritual directors.

If you read this book, remember the duty that you find to belong to the ministers and that also belongs to you. For it cannot be our duty to teach catechism and advise, if it be not yours to hear, learn, and seek advice.

As William Gurnall has exhorted us in his book, *The Christian in Complete Armour*, seek out your teachers and do not expect them to come to you. "For I confess that it is not small unhappiness to some of us who have to deal with the multitude, that we have neither the time nor the strength to speak to every single person in our congregations and attend upon them as their needs require. But let us look to it, that though we cannot do to the best what we would like to do, we may not be found wanting in what we may be able to do. But if once our hearts are filled with zeal for God, and compassion fills us for our people's souls, then we would be up and doing."

THE BIBLICAL CHARGE TO ALL

The theme of this book is contained in the words of Acts 20:28. "Take heed therefore to yourselves, unto all the flock, over which the Holy Ghost has made you overseers, to feed the church of God, which He has purchased with His own blood."

Although some may think that Paul's exhortation to these elders proves him to be their ruler, we really teach each other as brethren. Passages such as Colossians 3:16 and Hebrews 3:13 remind us to exhort each other daily. We do so, then, whether teachers or brethren, without any sense of supremacy of power or degree. We have the same sins to kill and the same graces by which to be quickened.

Had the bishops and teachers of the church thoroughly learned this short exhortation, how happy we would have been for the church and for them!

A twofold duty is contained in Paul's admonition. A four-fold motive is described to enforce it.

The first duty is to take heed to themselves. The second duty is to take heed to all the flock. The main work of the flock that is thus to be done heedfully is to feed them or to be shepherd for them.

The motives closely related together are these:

- It is their office to be overseers of the flock.
- It is the Holy Spirit whose authority has called them to be such.
- It is the church of God whose dignity is their object of devotion.
- It is the tender regard of Christ, whose blood has purchased them.

As elders, the Holy Spirit qualified those spoken of in Acts 20:28 with such gifts as made them fit to act accordingly. The Holy Spirit also directed the minds of those who ordained the overseers to such a task in that particular church, namely Ephesus. It is plain then, if the flock is to be overseen, no church should be larger in size than the pastors can personally supervise, so that they may "take heed to all the flock."

Then let able, faithful men be the overseers, who will make the Word of God their rule. If only would-be leaders of the church might be contented with the sufficient Word of God and not impose new canons and authorities over it, then I would not disobey such a bishop.

In further discussions on this text, I will pursue the following tasks:

First, I will look at the character of the pastor.

Second, I want to consider what it is to take heed to ourselves and how we must do it.

Third, I will show why we must take heed to ourselves.

Fourth, I propose to inquire what it is to take heed to all the flock of God and how we must do it.

Fifth, I will outline some of the motives why we should take heed to all the flock of God.

Finally, I plan to discuss some practical directions for managing pastoral work, as well as some of the difficulties of this work.

CHAPTER 2

THE CHARACTER OF THE PASTOR AND OUR FELLOWSHIP WITH OTHER PASTORS

A biblical charge to all having been given, let us concentrate on the manners of the pastor. There are twelve major characteristics that we may outline.

THE CHARACTER OF THE PASTOR

1. Purity of motive

Ministerial work must be done purely for God and for the salvation of His people. It can never be done for any private gain of our own. A wrong motive that aims at a wrong goal may well spoil the whole ministry, however good it may be in itself. For then it is not serving God, but ourselves.

Self-interest is a bad trade to choose. Thus self-denial is absolutely necessary for every Christian. But it is doubly necessary for a minister of the Gospel, because he has to have a double dedication and sanctification to God. Without self-denial he cannot serve God even for one hour.

Hard studies, much knowledge, and excellent preaching are

more glorious but still hypocritical sins when they are done for our glory. The saying of Bernard of Clairvaux is commonly known: "There are those who desire to acquire knowledge for its own value—and this is a base vanity. But there are others who desire to have it to edify others—and this is charity. And there are others who desire it so that they may be edified—and this is wisdom" (*Song of Solomon*, 26).

2. Diligence and hard work

The work of the ministry must be done with much diligence and effort, for it is of infinite importance to others and to ourselves. It is our task to save ourselves and others from temptation, to overcome the Devil, to demolish his kingdom, and to set up the kingdom of God. It is our duty to help others attain eternal glory.

These are vast works to be done, so how could these works be done with careless hands and minds? See then that this work be done with all your might. Study hard, for the well of spiritual knowledge is deep, and our brains are shallow.

Labor especially to practice and exercise your knowledge. Let Paul's words ring in your ears continually: "Necessity is laid upon me, and woe is me if I preach not the Gospel" (1 Cor. 9:16).

Consider then what lies in your hands. For if I do not bestir myself, Satan may prevail, and the Gospel perish forever, and their blood will be required of me. As Bernard of Clairvaux again says, "Those who do not engage in the work of men will surely be engaged in the work of devils." And as Gregory the Great says, "As many labors as you show for the sake of the truth, so many pledges do you also expect." For no one has ever been a loser by serving God in God's way.

3. Prudence and efficiency

This work must also be done prudently, orderly, and systematically. Milk must be given before strong meat. The foundations must be laid before we begin to build. Children must not be treated as if they were adults. People must be brought into a state of grace before we can expect them to do the works of grace.

The work of conversion, of repentance from dead works, and of faith in Christ must be taught first and in a frequent and thorough manner. The stewards of God's household must give to each their portion in due season. We must never go beyond the capacities of our people, nor should we teach Christian maturity to those who have not yet learned the first lesson.

As Augustine says, "If an infant is nourished according to its strength, it will be able to take in more as it grows. But if we exceed what a babe is able to take, then its strength will decrease rather than increase." Gregory has also said, "Just as we do not teach infants the advanced principles of science, but first of all teach them the alphabet and then sentences, so also the doctors of the church must first teach their congregations the basic doctrines of faith, and then only by degrees unfold the deeper and more mysterious issues."

That is why the church has taken so much trouble with its catechumens before it baptizes them. For it did not want to lay unpolished stones into a building, as John Chrysostom points out in one of his homilies.

4. Certainty about basic doctrines

We must also emphasize the certainty with which we teach our basic doctrines. The rest we can deal with less frequently. To teach Christ to our people is to teach everything. So see that they get to heaven and that they will have enough knowledge for this purpose.

Thus the great and commonly acknowledged truths are those that men live by, and which are the great instruments that raise men's hearts to God. These are they that destroy men's sins. Focus then on those central truths, and you will avoid frivolous details, needless decor, and unprofitable controversy. Rather remember the one thing that is needful. Other truths may be desirable, but these *must* be known.

Necessity is a great planner of time. If we are sufficient for everything, we might well take up the whole encyclopedia. But life is short and we are limited. So a focus on the eternal verities and the way souls are dependent on our teaching is precious.

I confess such limitations have determined my timetable and my priorities of time and studies. They help determine the books that I should read and the text that I should choose for my sermon. As Xenophon said, "There is no better teacher than necessity, which teaches everything most diligently."

This is why a preacher must often focus upon the same things, because the essentials are few. Do not therefore be tempted by novelties. Yet we must loathe the essentials with a variety of expressions. So often the wordy and tedious controversies that so waste our time and trouble us are made up of opinions rather than the essential truths. As Gregory Nazianzus says, "Essentials are common and obvious. It is the superfluities over which we waste time, laboring for and complaining that we did not achieve them."

Ministers, then, need to be observant in order to know for the sake of their flock what are the priorities. Likewise, in your reading, will you not choose authors who speak the truth plainly—even bluntly so—rather than those who speak eloquently but falsely? I purpose myself to follow Augustine's counsel when he said, "I would rather have speeches that are true than those which contain merely nice distinctions. Just as I would rather have my friends who are wise than merely those who are handsome."

5. Plain and clear teaching

All our teaching must be as plain and evident as we can make it. He who would be understood must speak at the level of his audience. He must make it his business to make himself understood. Truth loves the light. It is most beautiful when it is most transparent. For it is a sign of an envious enemy to hate the truth. It is a sign of a hypocrite to do this under the pretense of revealing it.

If it is not your object to teach, what are you doing in the pulpit? And if your object is to teach, why not speak in such a manner that you will be understood? There is no better way to make a good cause prevail than to make it as plainly and as universally and as thoroughly understood as possible. To be unclear is to show that you have not really digested the subject matter well.

Yet truth does require the capacity to receive it. So some cannot understand certain truth, even if you were to express it as plainly as possible.

6. Dependence upon God and docility before others

Our whole work must also be carried on in a humble sense of our own insufficiency. We need a pious, believing dependence upon Christ for all things. We must go to Him for light, life, and strength. For it is He who sends us into our work. When we feel that our own faith is weak and that our hearts are growing dull and unsuitable to such a great work as we have to do, we must have recourse to the Lord who sends us.

So we ask, "Lord, will you send one like me who has an unbelieving heart to persuade others to believe? Must I plead daily and earnestly with sinners about eternal life and death, and yet I have no real belief and feelings for these weighty matters? When you see, Lord, how naked and unprepared I am for such a work, prepare me with the resources for such a task."

Augustine remarked, "A preacher must labor to be heard with understanding, with willingness, and with obedience. Let him not doubt that he will effect this with fervent prayers more than with all the power of his oratory. By praying for himself and his audiences he will be fit to be a petitioner before he is a teacher. So when he comes and when he goes, let him raise his voice to God, and lift up his soul in fervent desire."

Prayer must carry on our work as well as our preaching. For he who does not pray for his people will not preach power-fully to his people. If we do not prevail with God to give them faith and repentance, then we are unlikely to prevail with them to believe and to repent. Thus Paul gives us frequently his own example, as one who "prays night and day" for his hearers. When our hearts then are out of order, theirs will also be out of order. If we do not prevail with God to help others, then our work will be in vain.

7. Humility
Our work must also be conducted with great humility. We must conduct ourselves meekly before all. When we teach, we need also to be open to learn from any who can teach us. Thus

we teach and learn at the same time. Do not let us proudly boast of our own conceit and disdain all who contradict us. Do not let us act as if we had reached the top and all the others had to sit at our feet.

Pride is a vice that ill suits those who would lead others in a humble way to heaven. Let us then take heed, lest when we have brought others so far, the gates should prove too narrow for ourselves. For God who thrust out a proud angel will not tolerate a proud preacher, either. For it is pride that is at the root of all other sins: envy, contention, discontent, and all hindrances that would prevent renewal.

Where there is pride, all want to lead and none wants to follow or to agree. Hence is the cause of schisms, apostasies, arrogant usurpation, and other forms of imposition. Hence also is the cause of ineffective ministry of far too many ministers, who are simply too proud to learn. As Augustine said to Jerome, "Although it is more fitting for the old man to teach than to learn, yet it is also more fitting that they should learn than to remain ignorant." Humility should teach us to learn willingly everything that we do not know. For if we would be wiser than all, then we must be willing to learn from all. For they who receive from all will become richer.

8. A balance between severity and gentleness

There must also be a prudent mixture of severity and gentleness, both in our preaching and in our discipline. Each must be admonished according to the context of the character of each person and situation that we encounter. If there is *no* severity, then there will be contempt of our reproofs. If it is *all* severity, then we will be taken to be domineering rather than persuaders of the truth.

9. A zealous and affectionate spirit

It is also important that we are sincerely affectionate, serious in our intent, and zealous in all our public and private exhortations. The importance of what we are commissioned to teach will condemn any coldness or sleepy dullness that we may be tempted to indulge in. Let us then be wide-awake. Let us then be in such a state that we awaken others.

Gregory has wisely said, "We should be like the cock. When he is crowing, he first of all sensibly claps his wings and strikes his side, in order to make himself more vigilant. Likewise, preachers, when they are about to deliver the word in public, should first exercise themselves in spiritual devotion."

Let us then, with much affectionate desire for our hearers, sharpen our words in such a way that we pierce even their stony hearts. For to speak coldly and slightly of heavenly things is much worse than to say nothing to them.

10. Reverence

Let all our work be done reverently, as becomes those who are conscious of the presence of God. We dare not use holy things as if they were commonplace. The more God appears in the midst of our duties, the more authority they will have before men. For reverence is that affection of the soul that comes from the deep apprehension of God. It reveals a mind that is intimately conversant with God.

But to show irreverence to the things of God is to reveal hypocrisy. It shows that the heart does not really agree to the tongue. The more reverent the preacher, the more he will speak as though he were looking into the face of God. Such a man will affect my heart much more deeply—though he uses very simple language—than someone who is irreverent and merely speaks eloquently. Perspiration is no substitute for inspiration. If fervency then is not also accompanied with reverence to God, it will have little effect on the hearers.

Of all the forms of preaching that I most dislike, I hate that which tickles the audience members with many jokes and entertains them with superficial amusement. It is as if they were in a theatrical performance, instead of being awed by the holy reverence of God's character.

Jerome writing to Nepotian said, "When you are teaching in the church, do not let the people be excited with a shout, but let them grow. For the tears of your hearers will tend towards true praise." We should see, then, the reality of the throne of God, with its myriad of angels in attendance there. This will keep us continually in awe of His majesty as we draw before Him in holy duties. This we must do lest we profane and take His name in vain.

So then all our work must be done *spiritually*. This we must do, as men who are before the Holy Ghost, and as those who have tasted of the things of the Holy Spirit. There is in some men a spiritual tone that godly hearers can discern and enjoy. While in others this secret touch is lacking, so that even when they speak of spiritual things, their manner is such that it is as if they were discussing common matters. So let all that we speak be spiritual, as from the Holy Scriptures, whereas what we quote from the Fathers is merely secondary and cautiously quoted.

With writers like Aristotle, the authority of these men is even of lesser value. For the wisdom of the world must not be magnified against the wisdom of God. Philosophy must be taught to stoop and to serve faith, while faith has the chief influence in our lives. Great scholars in the school of Aristotle must take heed not to glorify their master too much. At the same time do not despise those below their intellectual achievement. Do not despise those who are less than they are in their intellectual ability. For while the intellectually gifted may be *great* in the eyes of men, they may be *least* in the kingdom of God.

As wise a man as any of them declared that he will glory in nothing but Christ crucified. As Gregory said, "God first called the unlearned, and then some philosophers. He did not teach fishermen by oratory, but He taught orators by fishermen."

The most learned men should ponder over this.

Let all men have their esteem, but compare none of it with the Word of God. We will not refuse their services, but we must abhor them as its competitors. It is a sign of a sick heart that loses its relish for the excellence of the Scripture. There is a common nature in a devoutly spiritual heart to the Word of God, because this is the seed that gives new birth.

The Word is the seal that makes all holy impressions within the hearts of true believers. For it has stamped the image of God upon them. Therefore, they must be like the Word and highly esteem it as long as they live. Augustine speaks of "a certain follower of Plato who said that the beginnings of John's Gospel should be written in letters of gold and placed in the most prominent places in all the churches." If a mere pagan could so value that which suited his own platonism, how much more should we value the whole of Scripture as being so vital to the whole of our Christian character and interest! God is the best teacher of His own nature and will.

11. A caring love for people

The whole cause of our ministry must also be carried on in a tender love for our people. We must let them see that nothing pleases us more than what profits them. We should show them that what does them good does us good also. We should feel that nothing troubles us more than what hurts them.

Jerome again writing to Nepotian says, "As Bishops be not lords but fathers, thus they must be relegated to their people as to their children. Yes, even the tenderest love a mother has for her child should not surpass theirs." As Paul says, we must even "travail in birth of them until Christ be found in them" (Gal. 4:19). Our children in the faith should see that we care for no outward thing—neither money nor credit, neither freedom nor life—in comparison with their salvation. Instead, like Moses, we should be willing to have our name wiped out of the Book of Life for their sake, rather than allow them to perish and not be found in the Lamb's Book of Life.

Like the apostle John, we should not count our lives dear to us, so that we may find our crown of rejoicing by doing the work of God for their salvation. When the people see, then, that you love them unfeignedly, they will hear what you say—they will bear whatever you ask—and they will follow you the more readily. And when a wound is given in love, it will be more readily accepted than when one issues a foul word that is merely given in malice or anger.

Most people judge the counsel they receive by the way they receive the affection of their counselor. See that you feel a tender love for your people, and then let them feel it by your speeches and see it in your dealings with them. Let them see that you spent and are spent for their sakes. Let them see that all you do is for their own sakes and not for your own end.

To this end, the marks of charity are essential, as far as your pocket will go. For mean words will hardly convince anyone that you have a real love for them. When you are unable to give, show them that you are really willing to give, if you had it. Show them at least some practical gestures of your sincerity toward them. As Augustine said in his commentary on Psalm 103, "If you can, give; if you cannot, show that you care."

Be sure that your love is not carnal, coming from pride; let it not be as from a suitor of self-esteem, rather than coming from a lover of Christ. Take heed, then, that you do not connive at secret sins under the pretense of love. So friendship must always be cemented by piety. For a bad man can never be a true friend.

If you befriend their wickedness, you will show that you are such yourself. So pretend not to love them, if you favor their sins, and do not truly seek their salvation. As Basil the Great said, "Only the holy, as God is holy, can have true friendship." For by conniving with their sins you show that you are at enmity with God. How then can you love their sins as brothers? For sins are their worst enemies. How can you be their best friends, if you aid such foes? Thus just as parents will correct the children they love, so God chastens every son.

12. Patience

Finally, the twelfth trait of a pastor is to have patience. We must bear with many abuses and injuries from those for whom we are doing good. When we have studied their case, prayed with them, besought and exalted them, and spent ourselves for them, then we may still need more patience with them. We can still expect that after we have looked upon them as our own children, there may be some who will reject us with scorn, even hate and contempt. They will cast our kindness in our teeth with disdain and look upon us as their enemies. They will do this simply because we told them the truth. Yes, even the more we have loved them, the more they will hate us.

All this has to be accepted, and yet we still need unswerving and unwearied desire to do good on their behalf. In meekness we must still persist in instructing those who oppose their own best interests. God may yet lead them to repentance. Even when they scorn and reject our ministry and tell us to mind our own business, yet we must still persevere in caring for them. For we are dealing with distracted people who will reject their physician. Nevertheless we must persist with their cure. He is indeed an unworthy doctor who will be driven away merely by the foul language of a patient.

When we tell people that the natural man does not receive the things of the Spirit of God, and that they are beside themselves in matters of salvation, then we must be ready for their reactions. Do not expect fools to respond gratefully like the wise. These are not things that all of us can say, yet we may have to face any bad reactions that come our way. For we may be reproached and slandered for our love. They may be ready to spit in our faces instead of being grateful for our advice.

Yet these are the kinds of trials we will have to accept as good pastors. They will test and see if the remains of the old Adam are still strong enough within us that our hearts will react in pride and anger. It is the new man in Christ who can respond with meekness and patience. How sad it is, then, when many ministers of the Gospel fall short of this test.

THE NEED FOR UNITY AND FELLOWSHIP
AMONG PASTORS

These twelve qualities that we have described are required of pastors as individuals. But it is also necessary for us to be united as fellow laborers in the work of the Lord. We need to seek the social virtues of unity and peace of the churches that we oversee. We need to be concerned for the well-being of the whole work of God. We need to strengthen the common cause that we all serve, as well as the welfare of particular members of our flock. That is, we need to have a wider vision for the further enlargement of the kingdom of Christ.

As ministers we need, therefore, to hurt when the church is wounded. Instead of being leaders of schisms, we should lead in the initiatives that prevent divisions and that seek healing. Day and night we should be devoted to finding ways to close any breaches that may develop. We must not only talk about church unity, but actually seek it and serve in its cause. We should not only look for peace, but should follow after its pursuits when it flees from us.

We need to keep close to the ancient simplicity of the original Christian faith and build our foundation on its original unity. We must abhor the arrogance of those who harass and tear apart the church of God under the pretense of correcting errors and holding to "the Truth." The sufficiency of Scripture, of course, must be upheld; but do not let others add anything to it.

We must learn clearly the distinction between certainties and uncertainties, between fundamental issues and speculative theories of explanation. Then we can clearly distinguish the fundamentals of the faith from those that are merely private opinions. The peace of the church depends on the former, not on the latter.

We need, therefore, a sound proof of historical theology to see the ways in which the church has struggled to maintain the truth. We also need to know the writings of the early fathers so that we may benefit from their clearer teachings and explanations. But none of these is in itself the basic rule of our faith or of our love in God.

We must also avoid the confusion of those who make no differences between verbal slips of the tongue and fundamental heresies. How tragic it is that there are those who tear their brothers apart as heretics before they have made any effort to understand them.

We must learn to understand the basic reasons for controversies and then reduce them to the point where we see the differences between genuine differences instead of just seeing the prejudices. Then we will refrain from making the differences worse than they really are. Instead of quarreling with our brethren, let us rather cooperate together against our real and common adversaries.

That is why it is important for ministers to associate and to enjoy friendships, as well as to cultivate correspondence. Let us therefore meet constantly to serve this aim of unity. Then we shall find that smaller differences of viewpoint will not interfere with our fellowship together.

We must do as much of the work of the Lord in unity and harmony as it is possible to do. [Such was the practice of Synods among the Puritans] not to rule over one another, and to make laws, but to avoid misunderstandings, and to consult for mutual edification. To maintain love and communion together is what the Word of God has commanded us to do.

If only all the ministers of the Gospel had been men of peace and of a catholic rather than a factious spirit, the church of Christ would not have been in the situation of division that it is in now. The notions of brethren and the Calvinists abroad, as well as the differing denominations here at home, would not have been plotting the subversion of each other. Their ongoing bitterness to each other only strengthens the common enemy. But it hinders the building up and well-being of the church that it should now be experiencing.

CHAPTER 3

THE OVERSIGHT OF OURSELVES

Let us now consider what it is to take heed to ourselves. Let us see what we must do. Let our hearts also attend to this task as we understand it.

First, we are exhorted to take heed to ourselves, lest we should be void of that saving grace of God, that we are offering to others. For it is possible to offer this grace to others and yet be a stranger to the effectual workings of that Gospel that we preach. We can proclaim to others the necessity of a Savior and in our own hearts be neglecting Him. We miss an interest in Christ and His saving benefits!

So let us take heed to ourselves lest we perish, while we call upon others to take heed of perishing! We can starve while we prepare food for others. In Daniel 12:3, the promise to "shine as the stars" is given to those who turn many to righteousness. It is on the supposition, however, that they first be turned to righteousness themselves. For their own sincerity in the faith is the condition of their glory.

It is possible that many a man has warned others not to come to that place of torment that they have hastened to themselves. Is it possible also that many a preacher is now in hell who has called upon his hearers a hundred times to use their utmost care and diligence to escape its dark destiny?

Can any reasonable man imagine that God should save him for offering salvation to others, while he refuses it for himself? Can he be saved when he tells others truths that he has neglected and abused himself?

Many a tailor can go in rags while making costly clothes for others. Many a cook may scarcely lick his fingers when he has prepared the most sumptuous dishes for others to eat. Believe it, brethren, that God never saved any man for being a preacher. Nor did He reject a man because he was not an able preacher. He saved a preacher because he was a justified and sanctified man.

Take heed, therefore, to yourselves first. See to it that you be the worshiper whom you persuade your hearers to be. Make sure first that you believe what you persuade others daily to believe. Make sure you have heartily entertained the Christ and the Holy Spirit in your own soul before you offer Him to others. He who bids you love your neighbor as yourself implied that you should love yourself instead of hating and destroying yourself—and others, too.

Second, we are exhorted to take heed to ourselves, lest we live with those actual sins that we may preach against in others. Let us see that we are not guilty of that which we may daily condemn.

Will we make it our work to magnify God? And when we have done so, do we dishonor Him as much as others? Will we proclaim Christ's governing power? And yet when we have spoken of this power, do we deny it and rebel ourselves? Will we preach God's laws and willfully break them? If sin be evil, why do we live in it?

If there be no sin, why do we dissuade men from it? If it be dangerous, how dare we venture on it! If it does not exist, how dare we tell men it is so? If God's threatenings be true, why do we not fear them? If they are false, why do we trouble men needlessly with them and make them frightened without a cause?

Do you not know the judgment of God? They who commit such things are said to be worthy of death, and yet would we persist in doing them? (Rom. 1:32). You who teach others, will you not teach yourselves? You who say a man should not commit adultery or be drunk or be covetous—are you such yourself? You who make your boasts in the law—do you not realize that in breaking the law you dishonor God? (Rom. 2:21–23).

What! Shall the tongue speak evil that also speaks against evil? Shall it censure and slander and secretly backbite while it cries down these behaviors and the like in others? Take heed then to yourselves, lest you cry down sin and yet do not overcome it in yourself. For as 2 Peter 2:19 reminds us, "Of whom a man is overcome, of the same he is brought into bondage." "To whom you yield yourselves servants to obey, his servants you are whom you obey—whether of sin unto death, or of obedience unto righteousness" (Rom. 6:16). Yes, it is easier to judge sin than to overcome it.

Third, we need to take heed to ourselves that we may not be unfit for the great tasks that we have undertaken to complete. He must not be himself a babe in knowledge who will teach men all those mysterious things that are to be known in order to be assured of salvation.

Oh, what qualifications are necessary for that man who has such a charge upon him as we have! How many difficulties in theology need to be understood! What fundamentals of the faith must of necessity be known! How many obscure texts of Scripture must be expounded! How many duties must be done, wherein we may fail if we do not understand clearly their character, their purpose, and their context! How many sins we need to avoid, which cannot be done without understanding and foresight!

How many sly and subtle temptations we need to expose before our people's eyes—in order to escape them! How many weighty and intricate cases of conscience do we need almost daily to resolve! Can so much work, and such work as this, be done by raw, unqualified men?

What strongholds have we to batter down, and how many there are of them! What subtle, diligent, and obstinate resistance must we expect to deal with in every heart! How prejudice blocks our way in seeking to obtain a fair hearing! Often we are not disputing on equal terms, but with children who cannot understand us.

We have distracted people with whom we work. We have willful, unreasonable people to deal with, who are still never more convinced than when they are silenced in their own arguments. When they give you no reason, they will give you their resolution. We have to dispute against men's wills and their sensual passions, as much as against their understandings. We have not one but multitudes of raging passions and contradictory enemies at once to dispute against whenever we go about the conversion of a sinner.

O dear brothers, what men then should we be in skill, in resolution, and in unwearied diligence, who have all this to contend with and to do? Did not Paul cry out, "Who is sufficient for these things?" (2 Cor. 2:16). Can we then afford to be proud and lazy, as if we were sufficient? As Peter says to every Christian when considering the charge, there should be the reflection of our character: "What manner of person ought we to be in all holy conversation and godliness?" (2 Peter 3:11) So may I say to every minister, seeing how all these challenges lie upon us, what manner of persons ought we to be in all holy endeavors and resolutions for our work!

This, then, is not a burden to put on the shoulders of a child. What skill every part of a work requires, and how much time it requires! I do not think preaching a sermon is the hardest part of our work. Yet what skill is necessary to make the truth plain, in order to convince our hearers! How hard it is to let the irresistible light penetrate into their conscience and then to keep it there and drive the truth home! How difficult it is to work the truth into their minds and to work Christ into their affections! How clever it is for the pastor to meet every objection raised and clearly to answer those raising them! How challenging it is to drive sinners to convictions so that they see there is no hope unless they be converted or unavoidably be condemned.

To do all this in a language and a manner appropriate to our ministry, and yet which is most suitable to the capacities of our hearers—this requires much art. All this and a great deal more is required for every sermon we preach with holy skill. So great a God whose message we speak should be honored by our delivery of it.

How lamentable it is then to have a message from the God of heaven—that has everlasting consequences to the souls of men—and yet to give this word so weakly! How unfortunate it is to behave so impudently, or communicate so superficially, so that the whole business of our God miscarries in our hands! When God is dishonored, His work disgraced, and sinners hardened rather than converted through our weakness and neglect, what a responsibility we have!

How many times have worldly hearers gone home jarring at the obvious and dishonorable failings of the preacher! How many sleep before us, because our hearts and tongues are all so sleepy! And we do not even have enough skill and zeal to wake them up!

Moreover, think what skill is necessary to defend the truth against those who oppose it and deal with those who argue against it. What skill then is needed to deal privately with one ignorant, poor soul about his conversion!

Will a common measure of holy skill and ability of prudence and other qualifications serve for such a task? I know necessity may cause this church to tolerate the weak. But woe to us if we tolerate and indulge in our own weakness. Do not your reason and conscience tell you that if you dare to venture on so high a work as this, you should spare no pains to be fitted to perform it? It is not now and then a random and idle exercise or taste of studies that will serve to make a sound man of God.

We can excuse ourselves from the necessary intellectual diligence by saying that the Holy Spirit must alone qualify and assist us in our work. Does God encourage us in such idleness? Does He miraculously give us knowledge by dreams when we are asleep? Or does He take us up into heaven and show us His counsels? Oh, that men should dare so sinfully to quench the Spirit by such laziness and then pretend it is the Spirit who is doing it!

God has required of us that we be "not slothful in business, but fervent in spirit, serving the Lord" (Rom. 12:11). We must provoke our hearers to be such people, as well as be such people ourselves. Therefore, brethren, lose no time: Study and pray, converse and practice. By these four ways your abilities will be increased.

Take heed, therefore, to yourselves, lest you are weak through your own negligence, and lest you mar the work of God by your weakness. For "as a man is, so is his strength" (Judg. 8:21).

Fourth, take heed to yourselves, lest you exemplify contradictory doctrine. Beware, lest you lay such stumbling blocks before the blind that you occasion their ruin. Beware, lest you undo with your lives what you say with your tongues. Beware, lest you become the greatest hindrance to the success of your own labors.

It hinders our work greatly when other men contradict in private what we have declared to them publicly about the Word of God. This is so because we cannot be there to contradict them and to show up their folly. But it will much more hinder our work if we contradict ourselves. If our actions become a lie to our tongues, then what we may build up in an hour or two of discourse can be demolished with our hands in a week. This is the way to make men think that the Word of God is merely an idle tale and to make preaching appear no better than prating. For he who means as he speaks will surely do as he speaks.

Thus one proud, surly, lordly word, or one needless contention, or one covetous action may cut the throat of many a sermon.

Tell me, brethren, in the fear of the Lord, do you have regard for the success of your labors, or do you not? Do you long to see it have effect upon the souls of your hearers? If you do not, why do you preach? What do you study for? Why do you call yourselves ministers of Christ? But if you do, then surely you cannot find within your heart the desire to mar your work for a worthless thing.

It is an obvious error for all to see in those ministers of the church who make such a wide gulf between their preaching and their living. They will study hard to *preach* exactl, and yet study little or not at all to *live* exactly. All the week long is little enough to study how to speak for two hours, and yet one hour seems too much time to study how to live all the week. They are loath to misplace a word in their sermons; yet they think nothing of misplacing affections, words, and actions in the course of their lives. Oh, how curiously I have heard some men preach, and how carelessly have I seen them live!

So, brethren, we have certainly great reason to take heed to what we do, as well as to what we say. If we be servants of Christ, we must not be speakers only, but must serve Him also with our deeds. "Be doers of the Word, that in our deeds we may be blessed" (James 1:25). As we expect our audience to be "doers of the Word, and not hearers only," so, too, we must be doers and not speakers only, lest we be "deceivers of ourselves" (James 1:22).

A practical doctrine must be practically preached. We must study as hard how to live well as how to preach well. We must think, and think again, how to compose our lives (as well as our sermons) as may best lead to men's salvation.

If saving souls be your end, brethren, then you will certainly attend to this goal out of the pulpit as well as in it. If it be your end, you will live for it and make all your endeavors reach for it.

MOTIVES FOR THIS OVERSIGHT OF ONESELF

Having shown you what it is to take heed to ourselves, let me next lay before you some motives to awaken you to this duty.

First of all, you have heaven to win or lose yourselves. This is your goal as well as leading souls to everlasting happiness or misery. Therefore, you should begin at home and take heed to yourself first. It is possible for preaching to succeed in the salvation of others without bringing holiness to our own hearts or lives. Many shall say at that day, "Lord, have we not prophesied in your name?" (Matt. 7:22), and they will be answered: "I never knew you; depart from me, you who work iniquity" (v. 23). How many have preached Christ and yet perished because they lacked a saving interest in Christ!

It is a tragedy that we should ever have so many books in our libraries that tell us the way to heaven, and that we should study the doctrine of eternal life, and yet in spite of all this— we miss it! We miss eternal life! How tragic it is that we should study and preach so many sermons of salvation—and yet fall short of it! We fall short because we neglect Christ while we preach so many sermons about Him, or we resist the Holy Spirit while speaking of Him, or we talk about faith while we do not sincerely believe, or we call for repentance and conversion while we continue in a state of flesh and sin, we have aspirations to a heavenly life while we remain in worldly and earthly pursuits ourselves.

God is no respecter of persons. He does not save me for the dog collar or the ministerial calling. A holy calling will not save an unholy man.

Do I need to tell you that preachers of the Gospel must be judged by the Gospel? They must stand at the same bar and be sentenced on the same terms. They must be dealt with as severely as any other man. Do you really think you can be saved because of your clerical profession? Alas, it will not be. You know that no position in life will serve to save you. Take heed, therefore, to yourselves for your own sakes. You have souls to save or lose as well as others.

Second, take heed to yourselves, for you have a depraved nature. Your sinful inclinations are like those of everyone else. However much we may preach against sin, it still dwells in us. One degree of sin prepares the heart for another, and one sin inclines the mind to yet another. As a spark in the beginning of a flame, and as a minor disease that may lead into one more serious, so there is an aversion to God within us. There is a strangeness that is irrational and unruly. Since, then, there are so many traitors in our hearts, is it not time for us to take heed?

Those of us who seem strongest—we are really weak. How apt to stumble we are! How small a matter will cast us down! How easily our passions and inordinate desires are kindled, by perverting our judgments or abating our resolutions, cooling our zeal, and dulling our diligence!

Ministers are not only sons of Adam, but also sinners against the grace of God. Our treacherous hearts will deceive us, at one time or another, if we do not take heed. Those sins that seem to lie dead will revive. Our pride, worldliness, and many a corrupted vice will spring up that we thought had already been weeded out by the roots. It is vital for us, then, to realize how weak we really are. Then we will be careful with the dieting and exercise of our souls.

Third, take heed to yourselves because you have greater temptations and more exposure to them than other men. Weaker gifts and graces may carry a man through a laudable course of life, but it is because he is not so severely tested. Smaller strength may serve for lighter work. But if you venture on great undertakings of the ministry, you will need great resources.

You must also look to come off with greater shame and deeper wounds of conscience if your work is more exalted. The workman must pay heed to the weight of his responsibility. We have seen by experience that many men who lived as private Christians with a good reputation and piety have gone under more pressure as they entered more fully into the faith's labors. And when they were taken up into more responsible positions that overmatched their strength, they found themselves disgraced. So, if you will venture into the midst of the enemy, and bear the burden and heat of the day, take heed to yourselves.

Fourth, take heed to yourselves because the tempter will make his first and sharpest assault on you. If you will be leaders against him, he will not spare you. He bears the greatest malice against the man who is engaged in working the greatest damage against him. He hated Christ more than any of us, because He is the "Captain of our Salvation." So Satan hates the leaders under God more than the ordinary soldiers. He knows full well what a rout he can cause among the followers if the leaders fall before their eyes. He smites the shepherds to scatter the flock.

Take heed, then, brethren, for the Enemy has a special eye upon you. You shall have his most subtle insinuations, his incessant attention, and his most violent assaults. As wise and learned as you may be, take heed lest he outwit you. The Devil is a much greater scholar than you are. He is a more able debater. He can transform himself into an angel of light to deceive. He can cheat you of your innocence or faith before you realize what has happened to you. For his bait is always fitted to your temperament and disposition of character. In this way he can always take advantage of you.

Take heed to yourselves also because there are many eyes upon you. So there will be many who observe your fall. If you miscarry, the world will also echo with it. It is the same as the eclipses of the sun in broad daylight—they are seldom without witnesses.

If you take the position of prominence in the churches, you may expect men's eyes will be upon you. Other men will sin without observation, but you cannot do so. At the same time you can be thankful for this mercy that so many are potentially watching you, for this will restrain you.

Although some may be ready to tell you your faults out of malice, all these circumstances do help to make you feel responsible. They help you avoid sin. But God forbid that we should do evil in public and sin willfully while the world is looking at us! "For those who sleep, sleep in the night, and those who are drunken are drunken in the night" (1 Thess. 5:7).

Take heed, therefore, to yourselves and to your works. Remember, the world looks on them. For the quick-sighted eye of malice is ready to make the worst of a situation. It exploits and aggravates what it finds. It divulges whatever it can to get maximum advantage for its own designs. How cautiously then we should walk before so many evil-minded watchers! Remember that "a city set on a hill cannot be hid" (Matt. 5:14).

Take heed to yourselves. Your sins are more emphasized in others' opinions. A great man cannot make a small sin. There are several reasons for this. In the first place, you are more likely to sin against knowledge because you are better informed than others. With so much more knowledge, how much more willfully are you likely to sin?

In the second place, your sins will reveal more hypocrisy

70

than those of other men because you have spoken so much against them. What a terrible thing when we study to say all we can against sin, make it appear odious to our people, and then are found living in sin, secretly cherishing what we have publicly denounced! What vile hypocrisy it is to make our daily profession to denounce sin and then to nurture it within our own bosoms! This is the badge of the Pharisees, "they say, but do not." Many a minister of the Gospel will thus be accused at the last by this heavy charge of hypocrisy.

In the third place, your sins have more treachery than those of other men. Because you may do God more service, you can also do Him more disservice. How often have you proclaimed the evil and danger of sin and called sinners from it? How often have you declared the terrors of the Lord? All this implies that you have renounced it yourselves.

Every service you have preached against it, every private exhortation, every confession of it in the congregation implies that you are renouncing it yourself. Every baptism you have celebrated and every administration of the Lord's Supper wherein you have called men to renew their covenant with God implied that you yourself were renouncing the flesh in the world. These acts proclaimed your engagement to Christ.

How often and how openly have you borne witness of the odiousness and damnable nature of sin! Oh, what treachery it is, then, to make such a stir in the pulpit against sin *if* you then nurture it in your own heart and give it the room there that God alone deserves! Yes, you have then even preferred it before the glory of the saints.

Many more aggravations of your sins might be mentioned. But lack of time obliges us to leave the matter.

Take heed, then, to yourselves because the honor of your

Lord and Master and of His truth and His ways lies on you more than on other men. The nearer men stand before God, the greater dishonor has He by our defaults. And these inconsistencies will be attributed more by foolish men to God Himself. The severest judgment was imposed on Eli and his household because they "kicked at His sacrifice and offering" (1 Sam. 2:29). "For therefore the sin of the young men was great before the Lord, for men abhorred the offering of the Lord" (1 Sam. 2:17). It was that great aggravation to "causing the enemies of the Lord to blaspheme" that provoked God to deal the more seriously with David (2 Sam. 12:11–14).

If you are real Christians, then, the glory of God is dearer to you than your own lives. Take heed, therefore, what you do against God's glory in the same way that you would consider your very lives. How dreadful to see men point the finger at you and to hear them say, "There goes a covetous minister, a secret drunkard, a scandalous man. He is one who preaches such strictness yet who lives as loosely as others. He condemns others in his sermons, but he condemns himself by his life and conduct. In spite of all his talk, he is as bad as any of us."

O brethren, could your hearts endure hearing men throw the dung of your own iniquities in the face of our holy God? Or in the face of the Gospel? Or in the face of those who fear the Lord? Would it not break your heart to think that all godly Christians around you will suffer the reproach of your misdoings?

If one of you, who is a leader of the flock, should become ensnared in a scandalous crime, there is hardly anyone who seeks salvation diligently who would not be grief stricken at hearing about your sin. They are sure to have this cast in their teeth by the ungodly, however much they lament and detest what has happened to you. The ungodly man will tell his wife, the ungodly parents their children, and neighbors and friends will say to each other, "These are your godly preachers. Now see what comes of all your stir. Are you any better than others? No, you are all alike!" Such words then are what you can expect the godly to suffer, simply because of your own misconduct. "It is necessary that offenses come, but woe to that man by whom the offense comes" (Matt. 18:7).

So take heed, brethren, in the name of God. Be careful of every word you say, of every step you tread. For you bear the ark of the Lord. You are entrusted with His honor, so dare you let it fall and be cast into the dirt? If you who "knoweth His will and approveth the things that are more excellent, being instructed out of the law; and art confident that thou thyself art a guide of the blind and a light of them which are in darkness, an instructor of the foolish, a teacher of babes"; if you, I say, should live contrary to your doctrine and by "breaking the law, dishonor God, the name of God will be blasphemed among the ignorant and ungodly through you" (Rom. 2:18–24) ... take heed.

Do you not know that the standing decree of heaven is simply this: "Them that honour me, I will honour; and they that despise me shall be lightly esteemed" (1 Sam. 2:30). Never did a man dishonor God but it proved to be the greatest dishonor to himself. God will find out ways to wipe out all that can be cast against Him. But you will not so easily remove the shame and sorrow from yourselves.

Take heed to yourselves, for the souls of your hearers and the success of your labors depend so very much upon it. Generally, God fits men for great work before He makes them His instruments in it. So if the Lord does not soundly work within your own hearts, how can you expect Him to bless your labors to effect it in other hearts? He may do it if He pleases, but you have cause to doubt whether He will. So I will now show you four reasons why he who would serve others must take heed to himself. For seldom will God prosper the labors of unsanctified men.

In the first place, how can it be expected that God will bless the labor of a man who instead of serving God is working for his own self-interests? This is the case of every unsanctified man. For none but the upright make God their chief end, or do anything heartily for God's honor. They make the profession of the ministry merely a trade to live by. They choose it rather than another calling because their parents chose for them to enter it.

Or they are a minister because it is an attractive job to have. It is a life that gives them more opportunity to furnish their intelligence with all kinds of knowledge. It is also a job that is less laborious. It is a career accompanied by some reverence and respect from others. It is attractive because it gives scope to the leaders and teachers, and it has others depend upon them and receive the law at their mouth. Or it is a popular job because it gives some security.

These are the reasons why they are ministers and why they preach. Were it not for these reasons, they would give up. How then can it be hoped that God will bless the labors of such people? For it is not God whom they preach, but themselves, and their own reputation or gain. It is not Him but themselves whom they seek to serve. No wonder God leaves them to their own ways. If their labors have no blessing, then what can they give on their own? For then the Word reaches no further than their own strength can take it.

In the second place, a pastoral ministry will scarcely be successful if one is not doing his work heartily and faithfully so. How can others believe him when he does not believe what he says and cannot take his own work seriously? Can such an unsanctified man really do the work of the ministry? He cannot. He may exhibit a kind of seriousness, such as comes from a common faith, or the general opinion, or from natural fervor, or for selfish ends. But the seriousness and fidelity of a sound believer who intends ultimately only the glory of God and of men's salvation—these he has not. O sirs, all your preaching and persuasion of others will be but dreams and trifling hypocrisy unless your work is done thoroughly for God.

Indeed, how can you call sinners to repentance and to come to God with serious fervor, if you have never repented yourself? How can you ask sinners to take heed of sin and to be directed toward a holy life when you yourself never felt the evil of sin, or the wrath of holiness? These things are never well known until they are felt, or felt until they are possessed for oneself. How can you have compassion in your hearts and tears in your eyes as you beseech sinners to repent, when you have never experienced a need for this in your own life? What! Can you love other men better than yourself?

A third aspect of this challenge is this: Do you think someone can fight against Satan with all his might, who is the servant of Satan himself? Will he do any great harm to the kingdom of the Devil when he is himself a member and subject of that kingdom? Will he be true to Christ who is in covenant with his enemy and has not Christ in his heart? This is the case of every unsanctified man, of whatever cloth his coat is made. They are the servants of Satan and the subjects of his kingdom. It is he who rules their hearts. So are they likely to be true to Christ who are ruled by the Devil?

It is disastrous that so many preachers of the Gospel have been the enemies of the work of the Gospel, which they preach. How many such traitors have been in the church of Christ in all ages! They have done more against Him under His colors than they could ever have done in the open field of battle against Him. They have spoken well of Christ and Scripture, and of godliness in general, and yet slyly and intimately they have worked to bring it into disgrace. For they make men believe that God's followers are all but a company of hypocrites or self-conceited fanatics. So how many wolves have been set over the sheep, disguised in sheep's clothing! Pretending to be Christian, they are not. If there were a traitor among the Twelve in Christ's family, it is no marvel that there be many such today.

A fourth aspect of this challenge of consistency is that people will not likely have much regard for the doctrines of those who do not live as they preach. How can one believe someone who does not believe what he says himself? So if preachers speaking of the necessity of holiness do not live a holy life, people will think rightly that it is only talk. Further, they will think that what you preach is really needless and that they may boldly do so as much as you do.

The worst result of all this will be the teaching of your people to think ill of those who are genuine and faithful ministers of the Word. Their reaction toward such will be, "You are so precise and speak to us so much of sin and its dangers, the need of duty, and make so much stir about such things. Why then is such and such a minister, who is as great a scholar as

THE OVERSIGHT OF OURSELVES

you are and as great a preacher as you are, able to play with the boys and leave us alone in our fun, never troubling our consciences as you do? So why frighten us about hell and damnation, when sober, learned, and peaceable divines can be quiet and live with us like other men?" These are the kinds of thoughts and talk your negligence will occasion in others.

Finally, reflect on the need to see that all success of your labors depends upon the grace and blessing of the Lord. God has promised to His faithful servants that He will be with them and that He will put His Spirit upon them and His Word into their mouths. God may, and sometimes does, do good to His church through wicked men, but He does not do so usually or prominently. Rather His normal way is to use His faithful servants.

CHAPTER 4

THE PASTOR'S NEED OF REPENTANCE

Our business as pastors, dear brethren, is to humble ourselves. For we have neglected to nurture spiritually, and to instruct personally, those who have been committed to our care.[1] We also need God's help in fulfilling our future tasks. Indeed, without forgiveness for past neglect we cannot expect strength for future endeavors. So God must first humble us if He would use us. Yet the sorrow of repentance can be without a change of heart and life. So it is here we may commence with our confession—the need for true repentance.

It is only too common that we expect our people to repent when we have not done so ourselves. What efforts we will make to see that they are humbled, when we remain unhumbled! How hard we may press them with our teaching, convictions, and emphasis to wring out of them a few penitent tears! Yet our own eyes remain dry, and our hearts are so little affected by remorse. If we would only spend half as much time to affect and amend our own hearts as we do with our audience, how different our lives would be!

In Scripture, we find the guides of the church did truly confess their own sins as well as those of the people. Ezra wept and cast himself down before the Lord in His house. He confessed the sins of the priest as well as of the people (Ezra 9:6–7; 10:1).

So did the Levites (Neh. 9:32–34). Daniel also confessed his own sins, as well as those of the people (Dan. 9:20). Job 1:5 recalls that Job did so. Read Acts 20 and compare your life with Paul's exhortation to the Ephesian elders, and see if your heart does not melt in contrition under the sense of your neglect.

It is a sad thing when we put our congregations to sleep by our preaching, but it is tragic when we put ourselves to sleep. How awful it is when we have talked so long against their hardness of heart and yet we have become hardened unto the noise of our own reproofs!

God does not cause us needless sorrow. His purpose is to recall us to remember our own sins—that these are most obvious—and set them right before God and in our own sight. Then God can cast them behind His back when we deal plainly and faithfully with Him in frank confession. If we cast any shame on the ministry, it is not on the office but on ourselves, by exposing what we are doing. The glory of our high office does not communicate any glory to our sins or provide it with some covering for our nakedness. For "sin is a reproach to any people" (Prov. 14:34).

So it is our business to be responsible for our own sins and to give God the glory and to open our sins before Him that He will cover them. For it is only he who "confesses and forsakes his sins, that shall have mercy, while he that hardens his heart shall fall into mischief" (Prov. 28:13–14).

When Christ chose only twelve apostles, He did so deliberately in order that they would be kept near to His person. In this way they might become familiar with His teaching, life, and miracles. Yet how ignorant did they remain about Him and for so long! They did not realize that He would die as the sacrifice for the sin of the world. Nor did they know that He would be buried, rise again, and ascend into glory. Nor did they realize the nature of His spiritual kingdom!

It is hard for us to imagine how such ignorant men could be in a state of grace. How often did Christ lead them both publicly and privately (Mark 4:34)! How He had to rebuke them for their unbelief and hardness of heart! Yet after all this, how strange remained the great mysteries of redemption to them.

There was Peter, who had been called "Satan" because of ungracious thoughts that would contradict the role of the Redeemer. There was Judas, representative of the pride that was experienced by them all as they contended for status. What shall we also say of the reality that all forsook Him, and even of their failures after the outpouring of the Holy Spirit?

What of the public contention between Paul and Barnabas that separated them? What of Peter, who so misunderstood the calling of the Gentiles, and of his compliance with the Jews, that he endangered the freedom of the Gentiles (Gal. 2)? What of the desertion of Paul in his suffering when he admitted, "I have no man like-minded who would care for their situation; for all men seek their own and not the things of Jesus Christ" (Phil. 2:20–21)?

What of the charges made against the churches in the book of Revelation (Rev. 2 and 3)? It is not likely that Archippus was the only man who needed to be warned to take heed of his ministry (Col. 4:17). Nor is it likely that Demas was the only man who forsook a persecuted partner and turned after the things of the world (2 Tim. 4:10). Nor was Diotrephes the only one who, loving the preeminence, made quarrel and dealt unjustly and unmercifully in the church because of that.

[Baxter surveys at length "the sins of the ministers of the

Gospel from the days of Christ till now" in the next twenty-four pages of his text. He speaks of the political manipulations at the great church council of the early Fathers, the bitter strife among the Fathers, such as the Bishop of Alexandria against Chrysostom; of Chrysostom against his contemporaries; of Jerome against Ruffinos, Chrysostom, and others; and of Augustine against so many heretics.

He speaks of the persecution of the Waldensians by the Roman Church, of the rivalries of Lutherans and Calvinists, and of the Marian persecution in England. He describes the scorn of those nicknamed "Puritans" who were imprisoned; the absence of pastors in many congregations in Britain; the silence imposed on leaders such as Arthur Hildersam, John Brightman, Theodore Parker, William Ames, John Dodd, and many more; and the lack of church government or discipline. These combined to create much carelessness in the churches. Baxter now turns to the *present state* of the church.]

The great sins we are guilty of shall not be enumerated here. So my failure to list references for any particular sin is not to be interpreted as a denial or a justification of it. Rather I shall consider it necessary only to cite a few examples that cry out loud for humiliation and speedy reform.

The public then no longer confined the word *Puritan* to the nonconformists but applied it commonly to all the nations who spoke seriously of heaven, of death, of judgment, and who devoted the Lord's Day to such issues. They only needed to reprove a swearer or drunkard to be dubbed "the Precisians" and become a byword.

And there is scarcely such a thing as church discipline in all the land. I never lived in the parish, I confess, where a single person was publicly admonished or brought to public penitence or excommunicated even for the vilest offenses. So the ancient discipline of the church was unknown. Indeed, it is impossible for many of the pastors to do so, had they decided to do so, because they must know their own congregations first.

So the question was not, "Who shall be the governors of particular churches?" but rather, "Is church government at all effectual?" Those who urged the need for church discipline were dubbed "Disciplinarians," as if it were a kind of heresy to desire discipline in the church.

The persecution against those who had such intent became so severe that many thousands of godly pastors and their families left England to go to the continent of Europe, and most of all to America. Thither went John Cotton, Thomas Hooker, John Davenport, Thomas Shepard, James Allen, Thomas Cobbet, Nicolas Noyes, Theodore Parker, and many others.

To mention these things as instances of injustice is not enough. But far worse was the immorality of the day, so that in place of such godly men, the church was full of men who called themselves pastors but who were merely drunken, profane men. The church should have been cleansed of these.

Because of this influence, any man who protested against the lawlessness of the church would immediately be jeered at as a Puritan. Thus it became a greater reproach to live as a man of God than to live in open profanity. It was as if the church were once more subject to the invasion of the Goths and the Vandals.

Yet, thank God, not all the prelates of the church miscarried justice. We have not yet surveyed such leaders as Bishop James Ussher and Joseph Hall, learned, godly, and peaceable men whose names are as dear to us as any men alive. But they, too, were maligned for their purity and soundness of faith, and they, too, were scorned as Puritans. Tragically, too many of the Puritans reacted strongly against such persecution, instead of being meek and gentle. So these reactionaries in turn scorned the meekness of men like Bishop Ussher.

So there is a need to settle our own quarrels, to be tolerant unto godly men who have retained episcopal offices, and not to give up hope for the future ministry within the church. Humiliation is needed, therefore, to heal the schisms and differences of conviction among all true pastors of the church.

CONFESSION OF OUR PRESENT SINS

[From the historical review of the sins of the church, Baxter now turns to consider four present sins of the church: pride, lack of union, lack of commitment to the work of God, and lack of church discipline.]

1. Pride

One of our most heinous and obvious sins is pride. This besets even the best of pastors, and yet it is the more hateful and inexcusable in us pastors than in other men. It is so prevalent among us that it is obvious in our conversation, our manner of life, our company, and our very attitudes before others. It is the basis for our reasons; it shapes our thinking; it determines our desires; it promotes our envy and bitter thoughts against those more prominent than we are, who are given celebrity status.

What a sly and subtle companion, what a tyrannical commander, and what an insinuating enemy is the sin of pride! It accompanies men to the tailor to choose their cloth and to measure their suit. It dresses us up and sets the fashion. How often it chooses our topics to talk about, and even our words!

God desires us to be as simple in speech as we can be, to inform the ignorant, and to be as serious and convincing as we can be, in order to melt and change the unconvinced.

But pride stands by and contradicts it all. It trivializes and pollutes; it dishonors our sermons as if it were a prince decked in the costume of an actor or a painted fool. It persuades us to speak to our people what they cannot understand and then to say what is unprofitable. It takes the edge from conviction, and it dulls the life of our teachings, using the excuse that we shall not be uncouth or unpolished in our speech. If we have a plain and challenging passage, it throws it away as rustic and inappropriate.

So when God charges us to have all earnestness, this cursed sin of pride dominates and controls all the most holy commands of God. It tempts us not to be mad in our utterance with such convictions, but to speak softly. Thus pride remakes many a man's sermons, and the end is not the glory of God but the advance of the satanic.

Having prepared the sermon, pride then goes into the pulpit. It sets the tone, shapes the delivery, and strips away any offense, to gain the maximum applause. The end result is that it makes men both in studying and preaching seek their own self-interest, and after reversing worship roles, they deny God instead of glorifying God and denying themselves. Instead then of asking, "What shall I say, and how should I say it, to please God best, and do most good?" pride makes them ask, "How shall I deliver it to be thought a learned, able preacher, and be applauded by all who hear me?"

Yet this is not all; there is more yet. Oh, that it should ever be spoken of godly ministers that they should be so set on popularity as to envy the roles and reputations of their colleagues who are preferred over them! This is as if God had given His gifts as mere ornaments and decor for their personalities. And that they should then flaunt their reputations before the world, treading down and vilifying those of their rivals who stood in the way of their being so honored! What shame that those who would be saints and preachers for Christ should be filled with such envy and so malign God's gifts—when He should have all the glory! They do all these things because they seem to hinder their glory.

Is not every true Christian a member of the body of Christ, so that each partakes of the whole? Does not every man owe thanks to God for his brethren's gifts, as well as being members of one another? Does not each have his end in the whole? For if the glory of God and the welfare of the church are not his own purpose, then he is not a Christian. What a fearful thing it is, then, that men should be so unafraid of God as to envy God's gifts and allow their worldly hearers to remain unconverted. Or that they should choose for the drowsy to remain asleep rather than that such a ministry should be done by another who is preferred over them.

Thus it happens that men will so magnify their own opinions, and are so censorious of any thoughts that differ with them even in a minor degree, that they expect all to be conformed to their judgment. It is as if they were the only rulers of the church's faith. So while we denounce papal infallibility, we have too many popes among us! We love the man who will say as we say, and be of our opinion, and promote our reputation. But he is ungrateful when he contradicts us, and differs from us, and deals freely with us in our mistakes, and tells us our faults.

We are so touchy we can scarcely be reprimanded, and so arrogant that we can scarcely be spoken to, and so spoiled like children that we cannot endure being criticized. Thus our indignation comes not from having written or spoken a matter falsely or unjustly. It comes from fear of being contradicted.

Brethren, I know this is a harsh and sad confession to admit. If we could hide it we would, but the whole world would know about this state. We have dishonored ourselves by idolizing our reputations. We print and publish our shame and tell it to all. May the Lord be merciful to the ministers of this land and quickly give us another spirit. For grace is a rarer thing than most of us realize it to be.

Yet it is by God's grace that we have some here, or elsewhere, who are humble, lowly, and exemplary to their flocks and brethren. It is truly honoring to God that they are so. But alas, this is not the case of all. Oh, that the Lord would find us at His feet, with tears of unfeigned sorrow for their sins!

The very heart of the Gospel is the need to be self-abased. The work of grace is only begun and sustained by humiliation. Humility is not a mere ornament of a Christian. It is an essential part of the new creature. It is a contradiction to be a sanctified man, or a true Christian, and not be humble.

All who would be Christians must be Christ's disciples and come to Him to learn; and their lesson is to be meek and lowly. How many precepts and admirable examples has our Lord and Master given us for this purpose! Can we imagine Him deliberately washing and wiping His disciples' feet in order to remain arrogant and lordly? Does not Christ relate with the down-and-out, and yet we avoid them as contemptible? We think none is fit for our society save the people of wealth and honor. How many of us are found more often in the homes of the gentry than in the slums of the poor, the people who most need our help!

Oh, what is it that we are proud of? Is it our bodies? Are they not like that of animals, as dust of the earth? Is it our graces? Why, the more we are proud of them, the less we have to be proud about. When so much of the nature of grace is humility, it is absurd to be proud of it.

Are we proud of our learning, knowledge, and talents? Why, surely we ought to realize, if we have any knowledge at all, how it should humble us that we know no more. If we know more than others, then surely we have more reason to be humble than others.

So our very business should be to teach the great lesson of self-denial and humility to our people and to show how unfit it is for us to be proud of ourselves. So we must study humility, preach it, as well as possess and practice it. A proud preacher of humility is, to say the least, a self-condemning man.

Yet how sad it is that so vile a sin as pride is not so easily discerned by us! For many who are the most proud judge it in others and take no notice of it in themselves. They have such arrogance, such domineering spirits, that the world rings with it. Yet they will not see it in themselves.

How then can sincerity mark us when we have such a measure of pride? When we rebuke a drunkard or a fornicator and state that he cannot be saved without repentance, have we not greater reason to tell ourselves we cannot be saved unless we become humble? Indeed, pride is a greater sin than whoredom and drunkenness. Humility is as necessary as chastity and sobriety.

See also how many pitfalls there are in the work of the ministry—the dangers of becoming selfish, carnal, and impious, even in the highest work of piety. The fame of a godly man is the same as the snare of a learned man. And woe to him who assumes the fame of godliness without godliness! Truly, I say, they have their reward. When it was the fashion to be scholarly and exhibit empty formalities, then the temptations of the proud lay therein. But now through the unspeakable mercy of God, it has been acceptable to give credit to practical preaching and godliness.

The temptation of the proud is to be zealous preachers and godly men. What a thing it is to be eulogized as the ablest and godliest man in the country! To be known throughout the land for the highest spiritual excellencies! Oh, my brethren, you need only a little encouragement to find yourselves with the proud, being induced likewise. How it turns your head to be thought of as the pillars of the church and to have men hang on your words and to be ruled by you! Therefore, be vigilant, and in all your studies be sure to study humility. "He that exalts himself shall be brought low, and he that humbleth himself shall be exalted" (Matt. 23:12). For I note commonly that almost all men, good and bad alike, loathe the proud and love the humble. Thus does pride contradict itself and rob itself of all glory.

2. Undervaluing the unity and peace of the whole church

Too often we find men who are averse to the unity of the church and who are jealous of it. If Roman Catholics tend to idolize the church, shall Protestants go to the opposite extreme, to deny it, to disregard it, and to be divisive? For it is a great and common sin to be a part of religion as a faction and to confine one's love and respect to a denomination instead of the church universal. Of the multitude who say they are of the Catholic church, it is all too rare to meet with those who are of a catholic spirit.

Men do not have a universal concern and respect for the whole church. Rather they look to their own denomination as if that were the whole. Lutherans, Calvinists, and their subordinate divisions will pray for the prosperity of their own party and rejoice and give thanks when things go well with their own denomination. But if others suffer, they have little regard for it, as if it were not any loss at all to the church.

How rare then it is to meet a man who suffers and bleeds for the wounds of the church universal and who takes them to his heart as his own sufferings. Likewise, how few there are who have really understood the true state of the sectarian controversies between various church groups, or discerned how many of them have been verbal, and have seen how many real causes there are for division! Only a few like John Davenant, or Bishop Joseph Hall—whose work *The Peace-Maker* deserves to be written upon our hearts—have so understood. Yet it is common for such to be viewed suspiciously as heretics for their efforts at peace and unity.

Most of the matters that keep us divided are our church government: its right form and order. Is the distance so great that Presbyterian, Episcopalian, and Independent cannot agree? If men's hearts were really sensible of the church's case and sought to love each other unfeignedly and seek unity earnestly, the creation of peace would be an easy task.

Instead, the story too often is of learned and godly ministers of the church who first of all disagreed among themselves and then led on their people in those disagreements! We will read and preach on those texts that command men to follow peace with all men and to live peaceably with them, and yet we are so far from its practice that we snarl at, malign, and censure one another. It is as if zeal of holiness were the antithesis of zeal for peace, so that holiness and peace were irreconcilable.

This we have seen to our sorrow. Instead of living with one another as one heart, one soul, and one mouthpiece (to promote each other's faith and holiness and to admonish and help each other against sin), we have lived on the contrary in mutual jealousies and drowned holy love in bitter contentions. We have studied how to disgrace and undermine one another to promote our party's cause. We have also drawn our people into these struggles, dividing and slandering one another.

The public takes notice of all this and not only derides us but also becomes hardened against all religion. When we try to persuade them, they see so many factions that they do not know which to join—and think it is better not to join any of them. Thus thousands grow in contempt of all religion by our divisions.

If you are offended by my harsh language, I can tell you I have learned it of God. You should be much more offended by such satanic practices. The Holy Ghost would teach us, "Who is a wise man, and endued with knowledge among you? Let him show out of a good conversation his works with meekness of wisdom. But if you have bitter envying and strife in your hearts, glory not, and lie not against the truth. This wisdom descendeth not from above, but is earthly, sensual, devilish. For where envying and strife is, there is confusion and evil work. But the wisdom that is from above is first pure, then peaceable, gentle, and easy to be intreated, full of mercy and good fruits, without partiality and without hypocrisy. And the fruit of righteousness is sown in peace of them that make peace" (James 3:13–18). I pray that you read these words again and again, and study them.

I know that matters of truth are not to be received upon our credit alone. Yet our credible examples may do much to remove prejudice and remove the blockages at the entrance of men's minds. They may thus procure a more equal hearing to the truth and thus be to the good of our people. [Here Baxter adds ten more pages of discussion about the ecclesiastical controversies of his day, which fortunately are no longer relevant to our circumstances.]

3. Lack of commitment to the work of God

The next sin that I shall mention is that we do not take our work for the Lord seriously, unreservedly, and conscientiously enough. I thank God for those of our profession who do so. But alas, the general situation, even among godly ministers, is that we do so with reservation and even negligence. How few there are in our office who are truly devoted to it and who have given all they have to it. Let me enumerate some of the evidences of which I see we need to confess.

a) It is common for us to be *negligent in our studies.* There are few who take the trouble to be rightly informed and fitted for further work. Some men have no delight in their studies, taking an hour here and there, and then as an unwelcome task that they are forced to undergo. They are glad when they can escape from its yoke.

What do we need to keep us close to our studies and to promote our painful search for the truth? Is it the natural desire to learn? Is it the spiritual drive to know God? Is it the consciousness of our great ignorance and weakness? Or is it the sense of the solemn duty that we owe our ministerial work?

This diligence is required all the more because so many who graduate from university are so young that they need much further nurture and sound teaching before entering the ministry. I would not discourage such youths from the ministry, if they are competently qualified and encouraged to desire earnestly the salvation of men. But I know this, that theology is a practical subject, so that the knowledge of it thrives best in practical courses. A hearty endeavor to communicate and to do good is not the least help to our proficiency in it.

Indeed, what a lot of things there are that a minister should understand. What a defect it is to be ignorant of them. How much we miss when we do not utilize such knowledge in our ministry! Many ministers only study enough to compose their sermons and to do little more. Yet there are so many books that could be read and so many matters with which to become acquainted.

Even in our sermons we are often negligent to study more than gathering a few points of data, and we fail to go deeper, to see how we can set these matters forcibly in the hearts of other people. We ought to study how to convince, and how to get inside people, and how to learn to bring the truth to the quick—not to leave it in the air. Experience tells us that we cannot be learned or wise without hard study, unwearied labors, and experience.

b) Moreover, if ministers are to do *the work of the Lord, it must be done more vigorously* than most of us do it. How few ministers preach with all their might or speak of everlasting joy or torment with conviction. Instead, we speak so drowsily or gently that sleeping sinners cannot hear.

What a tragedy it is, then, to hear a minister expand doctrines and yet let them die in his people's hands for the lack of a relevant and living application. Could we speak coldly of God and of men's salvation? So, in the name of God, brethren, labor to waken your own hearts before you come and are fit to awaken the hearts of sinners.

If you give the holy things of God the highest eloquence of words, and yet do so coldly, you will contradict by your manner what you say of the matter. It is indeed a kind of contempt to speak of great matters without the appropriately great affection and fervency that they deserve. If we are commanded, "whatever our hands find to do, do it with all our might," then certainly such a work as preaching for the salvation of men should be "done with all our might"! Alas, how few there are who do so! Here or there, you see one or two who are so earnest and zealous in their preaching that people really are challenged by them.

c) If we are all heartily devoted to the work of God, we would also have *compassion on poor and unprovided congregations around us.* We could seek to help them in imaginative ways. For instance, we could establish a lectureship in the more ignorant parts of the country that would help purposely to establish the work of conversion. This could be done by the more dynamic preachers, who could substitute for the absence of locally able men.

4. Lack of church discipline

The negligence of recognized duties only reveals that we are not wholly devoted to our work as we should be. If there is a need of reformation among us, how many will do as little as they can to get by? If there are church duties to perform, how

many neglect them to get on with their own private busi-
nesses? So when we should meet to discuss the business of the
Lord, this one or that one will have affairs to do that have priority over God's business. And when God's work proves difficult or costly, how backward we are to do it and to make all
sorts of excuses!

Take discipline in the church. What has been talked about
or prayed over more in the past few years? Yet when it
comes to its exercise and practice, most of us do nothing
about it. How many ministers in the church do not even
know the members of their own congregations? What use is
all our talk about discipline, if our members never see us
exercise it practically?

Objections are that we shall be hated by all if we put discipline into practice. Men will not hear us if we do so. Therefore,
they would not do what we tell them to do if they refuse to
hear us. To these objections I give four answers.

First, Christ came not to give the world's peace but His
peace. He foretold that the world would hate us. Could not
martyrs like John Bradford or Bishop John Hooper, or any
other burned at the stake in Mary Tudor's day, have made the
same excuse? They could have argued we shall be hated and
exposed to the flames if we acknowledge the Reformation.

What is it but hypocrisy to shrink from sufferings and to
select only the easy and safe ministries to perform in order to
escape sufferings? But if you cannot suffer for Christ's sake,
why did you put your hand to the plow? Did you not first sit
down and count your costs? This makes the work of the ministry so unfaithfully done, because it is done in so worldly a
fashion. Men enter upon it as a life of ease, honor, and respect
from men and therefore resolve to attain their ends and have

what they expected by right or wrong. They did not anticipate hatred and suffering, and so they avoid them even if it means avoiding doing the work itself.

Second, in answer to the objection that we are incapable of doing good to the ungodly, I reply that God will bless His own ordinances to do good. Otherwise He would not have appointed them. If you admonish and publicly rebuke the scandalous and call men to repentance and cast out the obstinate, you may do good to many whom you reprove and possibly even to those you excommunicated.

I am sure excommunication is God's means. It is His last means, when reproofs do no good. It is wrong, therefore, to neglect the last means. However, those within the church's fellowship and those outside may receive good by it, even if the offender receives none.

God will be honored when His church is manifestly seen to be different from that of the world. It is also important not to confuse the heirs of heaven or hell. And we should not let the world think that Christ and Satan are not in conflict, having the same inclination to holiness or to sin.

Third—because of this second objection—I would like to know, "Should not all discipline be taken from the church?" On what grounds? Is this not against discipline itself, and not just the time and context of it? Wicked men will always storm against the means of their public shame. The use of church censure is purposely to shame them, that sin may be shamed. What age, then, since the apostolic times has the discipline been denied that you now want to eliminate? And if discipline itself is so intolerable to exercise, why have you sought it, prayed for it, and disputed over it as you have done?

Fourth, the conclusion must be that discipline is not such a useless thing as men make it out to be. I can speak from personal experience of it myself, that it is not undertaken in vain. But I know the pinching reason behind their complaints. They wanted discipline to be established and imposed by the secular power and not the church. But if we are Christ's ambassadors, sent to speak in His name, how can we do it in another prince's name?

There are times when we may have to preach against the civil authorities themselves. Does it mean that you will only preach when you have the permission of the authorities and when you are driven to do so by them? No one is hindering you from being both ruler and pastor over your churches. But to the shame of most of the ministers in England, we have freedom to do the work of Christ, and yet it is not done.

It is a sad inclination of the state of our carnal hearts when men can do so much more with us than God can. How sad it is that we will obey the commands of men, but we will not obey the commands of Christ. Is such a one fit to be Christ's servant and yet will not accept His commands as obligatory?

[Here Baxter points out an abuse of his time: Pastors were accepting their role in the hands of the civil authorities, rather than exercising it within the church.] I confess, I see in some ministers little of the fire of divine love, Christian charity, and compassion, and no heavenly mindedness or humble sense of their own weaknesses. Instead, there is too much of that other zeal that the apostle James describes, which blazes like a fire, and makes them full of suspicions, jealousies, censoring, and backbiting their own brethren (James 3:14–15). They live in plain envy and malice of each other instead of with Christian love and peace.

The prevalence of worldly and carnal interest works in a threefold way against the interest and work of Christ.

First, there is the compromise with worldly affairs, when one takes advantage of all secular opportunities and gains. This is not a private malady but one of epidemic proportions.

Just as in the day of Constantine, how prevalent were the orthodox? They were nearly all turned Arians, so that very few of the bishops did not apostasize or betray the truth. Today the same spirit is among us, so that our enemies sneer at us, saying that reputation and advancement are our religion and reward.

Second, there is the involvement in worldly business. How little care is taken of the church! How commonly are its duties neglected! I find money is too strong an argument for some men to resist it. I say all this. But what is more, if it were so deadly a sin in Simon Magus to offer to *buy* the gift of God with money, what is it to *sell* His gifts, His cause, and the souls of men for money? What reason have such men to fear lest their money perish with them!

Third (and this I have most to say about), if worldly and carnal interests did not prevail against the interest of Christ and His church, surely most ministers would be more fruitful in good works and lay out more of what they have for the Master's use. For experience proves fully that the works of charity do powerfully remove prejudice and open the ears to words of piety. If men see that you are accustomed to do good, they will believe the more readily that it is good that you desire them to seek.

But, brethren, this is not just ordinary charity that is expected of you. You must, in proportion to your talents, go beyond them. I know you cannot give away what you do not possess. I know also the great objection raised is that you provide for your wife and children and do not leave them beggars. There are few texts of Scriptures that have been more abused than the one, "He that provideth not for his own, and specially for those of his family, hath denied the faith and is worse than an infidel" (1 Tim. 5:8). This is made a pretense for greed. The words following that verse indicate it is the present provision and not future portions that the apostle had in mind.

You may educate your children as others do, so that they are capable of being most serviceable to God. But do not leave them rich, or forbear necessary works of charity, merely to leave them a larger inheritance. There must be some proportion kept between our provision for our families, for the church, and for the poor. A truly charitable, self-denying heart that has devoted himself and all he has to God is the best judge of the proportions to be given. Such a one is able to see which division of moneys is likely to give God the greatest service.

I confess that I hesitate to exhort men too strongly. I worry that they may fail from setting too high a standard and wound themselves. But it is hard to see how few men mortify themselves for the strong desires of the flesh, in order to live a single, freer life, without the temptations of wife and children. If he who does not marry is not better than he who does, surely ministers should labor to do what is best for them.

So if some are called to the celibate life, we should encourage and help such. This is one of the central points of Roman Catholic polity, that all bishops, priests, and other religious orders shall remain celibate. It is a pity that we cannot for a better reason imitate them in wisdom and self-denial, in the points where it can be done.

I would put no man to extremes. But a man who would preach of an immortal crown of glory must not seek after such transitory vanity. He who preaches of the contempt of riches must himself have contempt of them and so show in his life. He who preaches self-denial and mortification must practice these before the eyes of those who hear him.

Oh, brethren, what abundance of good works are before us, and how few of them do we undertake to do! I know the world expects more of us than we do ourselves. But if we cannot answer the expectations of the unreasonable, let us do what we can to answer the expectations of God, of our own consciences, and of all just men. For it is the will of God that with well-doing we should put to silence the ignorance of foolish men.

I shall go no further with the details of these failings and confessions that need exposing. But consider plainly that the great and lamentable sin of ministers of the Gospel is that *they are not fully devoted to God.* They do not give themselves up wholly to the blessed work they have undertaken to do.

Is it not true that flesh-pleasing and self-seeking interests —distinct from that of Christ—make us neglect our duty and lead us to walk unfaithfully in the great trust that God has given us? Is it not true that we serve God too cheaply? Do we not do so in the most applauded way? Do we not withdraw from that which would cost us the most suffering? Does not all this show that we seek earthly rather than heavenly things? And that we mind the things that are below? While we preach for the realities that are above, do we not idolize the world?

So what remains to be said, brethren, but to cry that we are all guilty of too many of the aforementioned sins. Do we not need to humble ourselves in lamentation for our miscarriages before the Lord? Is this not *taking heed to ourselves?*

NOTES

[1] This book originated in a Day of Humiliation, December 4, 1655, when men purposed to wait upon God in penitence for pastoral neglect and to ask for special assistance that the work of the Lord might be undertaken. It was a day set aside for intercession and earnest prayer for their pardon.

PART II

LOOKING OUT FOR THE FLOCK

CHAPTER 5

THE OVERSIGHT OF THE FLOCK

Having shown you what it is to take heed to yourselves, I shall now show you what it is to "take heed to all the flock." For it was necessary to consider *what we must be*, and *what we must do for our souls*, before we consider what must be done for others. "Lest one, while healing the souls of others, should catch the disease himself through a neglect of his own safety. Or, while helping his neighbors, he should neglect himself or fall while raising others."

THE NATURE OF THIS OVERSIGHT

It is implied, first of all, that every flock should have its own pastor (one or more), and every pastor have his own flock. It is the will of God that every church should have its own pastors and that all Christ's disciples "know them that labor among you, and are over you in the Lord, and admonish you" (1 Thess. 5:12).

The universal church of Christ must consist of particular churches guided by their own overseers. Every Christian should be a member of one of the churches, except those who, for special reasons, cannot join a body of believers. "They ordained for themselves elders in every church" (Titus 1:5).

Now the size of the flock should be determined by the number of shepherds. *All* cannot be shepherded without enough pastors in a church, or a small enough congregation to look after personally. God does not impose natural impossibilities upon us. Does God then require of a bishop that he takes charge of a whole county or of so many parishes or thousands of souls that he is clearly incapable of looking after? Is it not therefore absurd for intelligent men to desire this ambition as a privilege? Happy is that diocese or parish where the bishop or elders can adequately supervise their flock.

Can such work be delegated to others? One may argue forcefully in this manner. But the nature of pastoral work is that it must be done by the pastor himself. It does happen that some pastors have larger parishes than they can cope with, and so they are not able to properly oversee all the flock. In such cases, then, a pastor must only undertake to do what he can do for them properly and not try to do more.

This work may be considered in four ways: (1) the ultimate purpose of ministry, (2) the character of the work done, (3) the objectives of the work, and (4) the work of pastoral ministry.

1. The ultimate purpose of ministry
The ultimate end of our pastoral oversight must be linked with the ultimate purpose of our whole lives. This is to please and to glorify God. It is also to see the sanctification and holy obedience of the people under our charge. To nurture our people's unity, order, beauty, strength, preservation, and increase must be our task. It is the right worshiping of God. This means that before a man is capable of being a true pastor of a church, according to the mind of Christ, he must have a high esteem of

these objectives. He must make them the great and only end of his own life.

A man who is not therefore utterly sincere as a Christian cannot be fit to be a pastor of a church. This is proved by his love of God. Is he so taken up with God and with pleasing Him that he makes God the center of all his actions? Does he live only to be well pleasing to God? While it is useful that a man know and teach the original languages of Scripture and have some philosophy, his true test of usefulness is whether he is wholeheartedly devoted to God. For no one can be sincere in the means of serving God if he does not sincerely have the ends in mind. So a man must heartily love God above all before he can heartily serve Him before all.

Nor is a man fitted to be a minister of Christ who does not have the proper public spirit toward the church. He needs to delight in its beauty, long for its happiness, seek for its good, and rejoice in its welfare. He must be willing to spend and to be spent for the sake of the church.

To be a pastor of a church a man must also set his heart on the life to come and regard the matters of eternal life above all the affairs of this present life. Above the trifles of this world, he must appreciate in some measure the inestimable riches of glory. For he will never set his heart on the work of the salvation of men unless he also believes and values that salvation heartily.

He is also unfitted to be a pastor unless he delights in holiness, hates iniquity, loves the unity and purity of the church, and abhors discord and division. He must take pleasure in the communion of saints and the public worship of God with His people. These reflect the true ends of a pastor. Without them, he cannot do his task.

2. The spiritual character of the ministry

Since the work of the ministry concerns the pleasing of God and the salvation of our people, its character is *spiritual*. It is not about temporal and transitory things. It is a vile abuse to secularize the church with immersion into the business of the world. Our true business consists of the following two things.

First, it is our business to reveal to men what is that happiness or chief good, which must be the ultimate good. Second, it is our business to acquaint men with the right means to obtain this end and to help them use these means. In the pursuit of this end, we must not hinder them.

The first and greatest work of ministers of Christ is acquainting men with the God who made them; He is the source of their blessing. We should open up the treasures of His goodness for them and tell them of the glory that is in His presence, a glory that all His chosen people shall enjoy.

By showing men the certainty and the excellence of the promised joy, and by making them aware of the perfect blessedness in the life to come in comparison with the vanities of the present life, we may redirect their understanding and affections toward heaven. We shall bring them to the point of due contempt of this world and fasten their hearts on a more durable treasure. This is the work we should be busy with both night and day. For when we have affixed their hearts unfeignedly on God and heaven, the major part of the ministry is accomplished. All the rest will follow naturally.

Having shown them the right objectives, our next task is to inform our people about the right means to attain it. Here the evil of all sin must be clear. We must show them the danger of evil and how much hurt it has already done to us.

Then we must unfold to them the great mystery of redemption: the person, nature, incarnation, perfection, life, miracles, sufferings, death, burial, resurrection, ascension, glorification, dominion, and intercession of the blessed Son of God. We must help them know also the meaning of His promises, the conditions imposed upon us, and the duties He has commanded we should fulfill. They should also be warned of the everlasting torment He has threatened to those who are impenitent and neglectful of His grace.

O what a treasury of His blessings, graces, and privileges of His saints that we have to reveal! What a blessed life of holiness and communion have we to recommend! How many spiritual duties have we to place before them, in which we can also direct them! How many precious spiritual duties have we to lay before them!

How much of our own corruptions and sinful inclinations, however, have we also to discover and root out! We have the depth of God's unfathomable love and mercy to explore, yes, even the designs of the mysteries of creation, redemption, providence, justification, adoption, sanctification, and glorification. We have also the depths of Satan's temptations and of our own hearts to disclose.

In a word, we must teach our people as much as we can of the Word and the works of God. What two volumes these become for a minister from which to preach! How great, how excellent, how wonderful, how mysterious! All Christians are disciples or scholars of Christ, and the church is His school. We are His ushers. The Bible is His textbook. And this is what we should be daily teaching to those in our care.

3. The object of our pastoral care

The object of our pastoral care is *all the flock*, as a corporate body and as individuals.

Our first concern must be for *the whole community* of the church. Therefore, the first duties are the public duties. As people tend to prefer public duties before personal ones, there is little need to say more about this.

But our second concern must also be for *individuals* in the church. We need therefore to know every person who belongs to our charge. For how can we take heed to them unless we know them? We should know completely those in our flock. As a careful shepherd looks after every individual sheep, or as a good schoolmaster looks after every individual student, or as a good doctor knows each of his patients—in these ways we should know them. Christ Himself, the Great and Good Shepherd, takes care of every individual. We are reminded in Luke 15 that He "leaves the ninety and nine sheep in the wilderness, to seek after one that is lost" (v. 4). Christ tells us that "even in heaven there is joy over one sinner that repenteth" (v. 7).

Likewise, the prophets were often sent to individuals. Ezekiel was a watchman over individuals. He was sent to say to the wicked, "Thou shalt surely die" (Ezek. 33:14). Likewise, Paul taught publicly and from house to house. He also warned "every man, and taught every man in all wisdom, that he might present every man perfect in Christ Jesus" (Col. 1:28). So, too, Christ exposed His parables to the Twelve apart.

We, too, must give an account of our watch over the souls of all who are bound to obey us (Heb. 13:7). Many more passages of Scripture assure us that it is our duty to take heed to every individual person who is in our flock. And many passages in the ancient church council do plainly tell us that it was also the practice in those days to do likewise. In one passage, Ignatius says, "Let assemblies be often gathered; inquire into all by name; despise not servant-men or maidens." So you see it was then taken as a duty to look upon every member of the flock by name, even if it should be the meanest servant-man or maid.

But you may object. How can one practically realize such a charge? Supposing you admit you cannot and need the assistance of others. Have you enough income for your family, let alone enough to share with someone in order to have other pastoral assistance? Is it not hard on your wife and children to live with less? Yes, one may answer. But are there not many families in one's parish that are living with less than you do?

For you see, there have been some who were willing to preach for nothing so long as they had the freedom to preach. But they ask further, Is it not better to live in reduced economic circumstances than that your parishioners are damned? Your bread is not more important than their eternal salvation, is it? Do my people live in ignorance, then, simply because I am reluctant to let my family suffer a little want?

While it is our duty to take heed to all the flock, we must pay attention to specific classes of people who need our help in individualistic ways. This is a matter often overlooked or imperfectly understood. So I shall discuss it further.

a) The work of conversion is the first and most vital part of our ministry. For there are those who are Christian only in name, who have need to be truly "born again." We may not be sure that this or that man in particular is unsound and unsanctified. Yet as long as there is a strong probability that there are several in our congregation who are in this category, we should labor with all our might on their behalf.

Ah, me! The misery of the unconverted is so great that it calls for our utmost compassion. They are in the grip of bitterness and as yet have no part or fellowship in the pardon of their sins or in the hope of glory. We are therefore driven by the necessity "to open their eyes, and to turn them from darkness to light, and from the power of Satan unto God; that they may receive forgiveness of sin, and inheritance among the sanctified by faith in Christ" (Acts 26:18).

I confess I am forced frequently to neglect those things that further increase the knowledge of the godly in favor of dealing with the lamentable necessities of the unconverted. Just as Paul's spirit was stirred within him when he saw the Athenians so addicted to idolatry, I am so moved by the plight of the unconverted. It seems to me that he who will let a sinner go to hell simply by not speaking to him gives less place to hell than the Redeemer of souls does. So whoever you pass over, do not forget the unsaved. I say it again. Focus on the great work of evangelism, whatever else you do or leave undone.

b) The next part of the ministry is the upbuilding of those who are truly converted. This varies widely from those who are young, or weak, to those who are in relapse, or have some other need. So all our work is reducible to five specific needs: confirmation, progress, preservation, restoration, and comfort. These vary with the needs of those who are nurtured in the faith, for there are many classes of Christians who need upbuilding.

First, there are the young and the weak. They may have been so for a long time. The latter condition is typical of many Christians, since most of them content themselves with a spiritually weak experience of the grace of God. Then it is very easy to make them more rigid about the truth. But increasing their knowledge and gifts is not easy. Increasing their graces is hardest of all.

The troublesome thing about being spiritually weak is that it exposes us to many dangers. It lessens comfort and delight in God. It takes away the sweetness of God's ways. Such weakness leaves us much less able to serve God and man. It brings less honor to our Master and our profession. It also handicaps us in doing less good to those around us. In spiritual weakness we are too easily seduced by the Devil. We are also less able to resist and stand in an encounter. We know less about ourselves and are prone to be mistaken about our condition. In a word: We are less useful to ourselves; we are a dishonor to the Gospel. Since spiritual weakness is such a sad specter, we should be diligent to cherish and increase God's grace in such a case. For the strength of the Christian is the honor of the church.

When men are inflamed with the love of God and live by a dynamic, working faith; when men set their hearts lightly on the profits and honors of this world; when men love one another with a pure heart fervently—then they are a witness indeed. What an honor are those who can bear and forgive heartily all wrongs done to them and who suffer joyfully for the cause of Christ.

What ornaments to the church are they who study to do good, who walk harmlessly in the world, and who are ready to be servants of all men. How beautiful are those who become all things to all men to win them and yet avoid all appearance of evil. When there is exhibited that proper balance of prudence, humility, zeal, and heavenly spirituality, non-Christians will sooner believe the Gospel is indeed the word of truth and power. For they see its effects upon the hearts and lives of such people.

The world is better able to read the nature of religion in a man's life than in the Bible. They who obey not the Word may be won by the conversation of such. It is therefore an essential part of our work to labor more in polishing and perfecting the saints, so that they are strong in the Lord and fitted for the Master's use.

Second, we need to promote the progress of the morally handicapped. For there is another category of believers who need our special help, and they are those who suffer the moral handicap of some particular disability that prevents them from developing more fully. They are vulnerable to particular temptations. This affects others, too. It is a pity so many are like this! Some are particularly addicted to pride, others to worldliness, and others again to this or that sensual desire. Many, too, are subject to sinfulness and other disturbing passions.

It is our duty to do what we can for all such people. We can help by discussion, by uncovering the odious features of their sins, and also by giving suitable directions about the remedy. Such words help them overcome their weaknesses. For we must be no more excusing of the sins of the godly than of the ungodly, or befriend one more than the other. We are leaders of Christ's army against the powers of darkness. And so we must resist all the works of darkness wherever we find them, even though it be in the children of light.

The more we love their persons, the more we need to express our grievance about their sin. Yet even here we must expect to meet with some who are very sensitive and hard to deal with. When sin has so developed in them that they are in love with it, this is especially true. Such people will be pettish and impatient when reproved, perhaps more so than those who appear to be in a worse state. They may complain that the minister who preaches against them preaches against the godly. What a heinous crime this is, to make God and godliness accessory to their sins! But the ministers of Christ must do their duty, in spite of all men's peevishness. They must not so much hate the brother as to forbear the necessary sin to rebuke him. Nor should they allow sin to lie upon his soul. Though it must be done with much prudence, yet it must be done.

A third aspect of our ministerial work is the preservation of the tempted. Those who have fallen into great temptations need much assistance. Therefore, every minister should be a man who has insight into the tempter's wiles. We should know their variety, the cunning craft of all Satan's instruments that lie in wait to deceive, and the methods and devices of the great deceiver. Some of our people are tempted by error and heresy, especially among the young, the unsettled, or the self-conceited. What holy prudence and industriousness are required of a pastor to keep the flock from being tainted with heresies! How vital it is to keep the flock from divisions and to promote unity and concord! This we can only do when we publicly maintain our own testimony and privately live with blameless and exemplary character.

Others may live with the temptation to worldliness, or to gluttony, or to drunkenness, or to some form of uncleanness. So some are prone to one sin, and some to another. A faithful pastor should have his eyes on them all. He should labor to know their natural temperaments, their situations, and the context of their affairs in the world. A pastor should be aware of the company they live with and deal with, so that he may know where their temptations lie. Thus he knows speedily, prudently, and diligently how to help them.

A fourth part of the ministry to the converted in our community is the need to seek the restoration of fallen Christians. Either they have fallen into some scandalous sin, or else their zeal and diligence have cooled, or they have shown in some other way that they have lost their first love. Since it is so sad to see them lose so much of their life, their peace, and their usefulness to God, we must do all in our power to bring about their recovery. Left as they are, they will become so much more serviceable to Satan and his cause! It is sad for us to see all our labor come to this and be frustrated when we have taken so much trouble with them. But it is saddest of all to think that God should so be abused by those He has loved and for whom He has done so much. It is tragic to think that the Enemy should take advantage of this situation and that Christ should be so wounded in the house of His friends.

Partial backsliding could be viewed as the precursor to total apostasy. The sadder the case of such a Christian is, the more obliged we feel to help in his effectual recovery: "If a man be overtaken in a fault, ye which are spiritual, restore such a one in the spirit of meekness" (Gal. 6:1). Do so in such a way that the wound is thoroughly probed and healed, whatever pain it costs. Above all, look to the honor of the Gospel. See that there is full and free confession that evidences true repentance. Seek some reparation for the church, for the wound of dishonor that such a man has given it by his sin. Much skill is required to restore him.

A fifth aspect of our work among the converted is to comfort the disconsolate. Giving a basis for peace in our people's souls that is sure and lasting is a vital ministry. To this end we need to know the character of the complainants and the course of their lives. For all people need the same consolations that have similar complaints. Since I have spoken of this elsewhere, and there is so much said by many others (especially by Mr. Robert Bolton in his *Instructions for the Right Comforting of Souls*, 1631), I will say no more here.[1]

The rest of our ministerial work is with the encouragement of those who are strong. For they also have need of our assistance. They need partly to avoid temptation like everyone else, and they, too, need to preserve what grace they have. They need encouragement to make further progress and increase their faith. They need to be directed in the improvement of their strength for the service of Christ. Knowing that their brethren, the aged, the tempted, and the afflicted need to be encouraged especially, the strong should do so that the weak may hold on and persevere to obtain the crown.

All these are the objects of the minister's work. In respect to each of these, he must take heed to all the flock.

4. The work of pastoral ministry

Let us now consider briefly the actual activities of pastoral ministry.

One aspect of the ministry—a most excellent one—is the public preaching of the Word. It is a work that requires great skill and especially greater life and zeal than any of us can ever bring to it. For it is no small matter to stand up before a congregation and deliver a message of salvation or judgment as from the living God, doing so in the name of the Redeemer. It is no easy matter to speak so plainly that the ignorant may understand us. Or to preach so seriously that the deadest hearts may feel us. Or to reason so convincingly that those who are argumentative may be silenced.

I know that there is a debate among us concerning the role of preaching. Preaching is indeed proper for a minister of a congregation. Preaching to the unbelieving world in other cultures of other faiths is a separate task. But preaching to the local church is clearly the role of a pastor.

Moreover, the master of a family needs to preach to his own family, as a schoolmaster does to his students. What is important to recognize is that there are appointed offices; each of these offices trains one to teach in the context of one's own appointment.

A second aspect of our pastoral ministry is to administer the sacrament of baptism and the Lord's Supper.

A third aspect is to lead in public prayers of the church and in praises to the Lord. Indeed, a large part of God's service in church assemblies consisted until recently of public praise and the Eucharistic acts of Holy Communion. The Lord's Day was still kept as a day of thanksgiving in hymns, the common rejoicing of the faithful, and in the special commemoration of the work of redemption. I am as concerned as others are about the necessity of preaching. But I think the solemn praises of God should take up much more time on the Lord's Day than is practical in most places. Indeed, this is an indication of how much we are magnifying the privileges of the Gospel, of how much we know about a life of love and heavenly joys, when we practice thanksgiving.

A fourth aspect of our pastoral work is the special care that we take of each member of the flock. [Here Baxter repeats what he has already emphasized—the necessity to know the personal needs, character, and inclination of individuals and the duty of instructing the ignorant and directing the consciences of the needy.]

We must also have a special care for families to see that they are well ordered and that each performs its duties. For the life of religion, and the welfare and glory of the church and state, depend much on family government and duty. If we neglect this, we will undo all. How can we see to the revival of a whole congregation if all the work is cast upon the pastor alone? Or if the heads of families neglect their responsibilities, what will be the extent of a church awakening?

If any good is begun by the pastoral ministry, it will be stopped—or at least hindered—if the family is careless, prayerless, and worldly. But if you get the heads of families to do their part, to take up the work where you have left off, and then finally to help it on, what an abundance of good might be done! So I urge you to see the importance of family cooperation in your ministry.

Your goal is to be effective in family ministry. So get information about how each family is organized and how God is worshiped there. Visit the families when they are at leisure; and find out if the head of the family prays within his home, reads the Scriptures, enters into worship in other ways. Labor to convince those who are negligent about the validity of such duties; ask that they promise to reform their ways for the future.

If you find some do not know how to pray for families, study their needs and guide them in how to develop prayerful lives. Perhaps those who have never learned to pray may begin by reciting set prayers from memory. See also what profitable and stimulating books may be read within the family (besides the Bible). Such works might include William Whately's *The New Birth* and John Donne on the commandments [both of which were popular in the seventeenth century]. [Baxter also adds a suggestion that a family unversed in these Christian practices might spend Sunday with a neighboring family that can nurture it in such godly habits and practices.]

Pay attention also to the humble, upright, and obedient Christians who may be vilified and treated badly by ministers who should know better. A pastor cannot expect his people to honor him if he does not give the love and respect to them that is due to all Christians as members of Christ.

Another aspect of our work is visiting the sick and helping them prepare for a more fruitful life or indeed for a happy death. When we see how vital the remaining few days or hours may be to the dying, we begin to see how important it is to look after them and to minister to them for their eternal state. So great is the change made by death that it should awaken our greatest sensibilities to have compassion and concern for their souls.

When the dying's time is almost gone, and they must now or never be reconciled to God, they are desperately concerned to redeem those hours. They are intensely occupied with the thought of laying hold of eternal life! And when we see that we are likely to have only a few days or hours more with them (unless we ourselves are unbelievers), would we not do all that we can for their salvation in that short time?

When a man is almost at his journey's end, and the next step brings him to heaven or to hell, it is time for us, while there is hope, to aid him all we can. For even the hardest sinners will hear us on their deathbed, though before they scorned us. As

Cyprian said to those in health, "He who every day reminds himself he is dying, despises the present, and will hasten toward the things to come. Much more so he who feels himself to be in the very act of dying."

Perhaps you will argue that these forced changes are not authentic and that, therefore, we have no great hope in them saying or doing good. I confess it is very common to be frightened into ineffectual purposes. Augustine illustrates this when he says, "He cannot die badly who lives well; and scarcely shall he die well who lives badly." Yet "scarcely" and "never" are not all one. So there are exceptions, those exceptions being individuals who are converted to their Savior (in the manner of the dying thief on the cross).

Since I did not intend to furnish a directory for the whole ministerial work, I will not stop to tell you in detail what must be done in their last moments. But notice three things.

- Do not wait until their strength and understanding are gone and the time is so short that you scarcely know what to do. Go to them as soon as they are sick, whether they send for you or not.
- When the time is so short, get to the essentials at once, and dwell on those truths that are most calculated to promote their conversion.
- If they recover, be sure to remind them of their promises and resolutions in time of sickness. Go to them purposely to set these things in their consciences. Whenever afterward you see them remiss, remind them of their sickbed experiences. As a bishop of Cologne is said to have answered the emperor Sigismund, when he asked him what was the way to be saved, "He must be what he

purposed, or promised, when he was last troubled with the stone and the gout."

We need also to reprove and admonish those who live offensively or impenitently. Before we bring such matters publicly before the church, we should seek to do so privately. A great deal of skill is needed in doing so according to the various tempers of the offenders. But with the majority of cases, it is necessary to begin with great plainness and power of conviction in order to shake their careless hearts and make them see that they cannot dally with sin. They need to see the evil of it; its sad effects; the unkindness, unreasonableness, unprofitableness; and all its other negative results. They must see what it is they are doing against God and to themselves.

This leads us to the whole question of church discipline. After the private reproofs are administered, there arises also the need for public reproofs: persuading the person to meet expressions of repentance, praying for them, restoring the penitent, and excluding and avoiding the impenitent.

[At this point, Baxter inserts a long discussion on the methods of exercising "church discipline." Much of this is omitted here because it is related to the conditions of his own time in the seventeenth century, rather than to our circumstances today.]

There are, however, biblical principles that apply to all of us at all times. The first is the need of public repentance. "Them that sin rebuke before all, that others also may fear" (1 Tim. 5:20). Such a "rebuke is with all authority" (Titus 2:15). Yea, even if it is an apostle who should sin openly, he, too, must be openly reproved, as when Paul said, "Peter ... I withstood him to the face, because he was to be blamed" (Gal. 2:11, 14).

If those rebuked are not repentant, then avoid them. "Withdraw yourselves from every brother that walketh disorderly" (2 Thess. 3:6). "If any man obey not our word ... note that man, and have no company with him, that he may be ashamed" (2 Thess. 3:14; 1 Cor. 5:11, 13).

For example, assume that a sinner is thus admonished and prayed for. If it please the Lord to open his eyes and to give him remorse, it is our duty to proceed to his full recovery—before we proceed to further censure. Do not either discourage him by too much severity, or make nothing of the discipline by too much leniency and levity—smoothing over it carelessly.

If therefore he has once sinned scandalously but his repentance seems deep and serious, then we may in some cases restore him then. But if he has long lived in sin, it is much better for him to wait in penitence on a convenient time before he is restored. When he is ready, assure him of the riches of God's love and the sufficiency of Christ's blood to pardon his sins. Then forget them as Christ does. Give thanks to God for his recovery, and pray for his confirmation and future preservation.

In the discipline of rejecting and removing from the church's communion those who remain impenitent after sufficient trial, note two things. (1) If a man has sinned once in a scandalous manner, it is but a profession of repentance that we can expect for our satisfaction. (2) If he be accustomed to sin, or has often broken his promise, then it is an actual reformation we must expect.

For those who remain unrepentant or even excommunicated, it is still important that we go on praying for their repentance and restoration. And if God should give them repentance, we must gladly receive them again into the communion of the church.

Would then we were faithful in the practice of this discipline! God's provision of discipline is reproached when we profess to be satisfied with its matter and manner and yet neglect its exercise. Shall we who are pastors not consider these things of greater importance? We are likely to face the heaviest charges concerning this matter, when we stand before the judgment seat of Christ.

There may be those who are so deluded as to reproach the need of any church discipline or who will hinder its exercise. But what of us? Have we vilified it by our constant omission of discipline while we talked about its need? How shall we cover up our hypocrisy? Should we shrug off the knowledge of our Master's will in this matter?

I believe the tempter has gained as great victory in getting but one godly pastor of a church to neglect discipline as he has in getting the same pastor to neglect preaching. As the impure used to reproach the diligent by the name of "Puritans," so do they reproach the faithful pastors by the name of "Disciplinarians." If only it were understood how much of pastoral authority and work really consists of church guidance. Then there would be so much less prejudice against the proper exercise of discipline. For to be against discipline is to be against the pastoral ministry; and to be against the pastoral ministry is to be against the church; and to be against the church is to be against Christ.

Was not Christ Himself the leader of these Disciplinarians? Did He not institute discipline and make His ministers the rulers and guides of His church? What would these men have said if they had seen the practice of the ancient church for many centuries after Christ, which exercised a discipline so much more rigorous than any among us do? They did this even in the heart of the heathen persecutions, as the Cyprian epistles reveal.

I know that the word *discipline* has been corrupted by legalism and by such austere impositions as: "Touch not, taste not, handle not." But it is that ancient and truly Christian discipline that is being contended for here.

NOTES

[1] In addition to numerous sermons on this theme, Richard Baxter also published *The Christian Directory; The Right Method for a Settled Peace of Conscience and Spiritual Comfort;* and *Directions for Weak, Distempered Christians.*

THE MOTIVES OF PASTORAL OVERSIGHT

W e now turn to consider the motives for our future ministry. We should not, certainly, be careless in ministry or in personal life as we have been in the past. [Here Baxter is thinking of the state of affairs in his county of Worcestershire. This was the reason for holding an original convention, to which he submitted this report in lieu of his presence.]

I. WE ARE OVERSEERS OF THE FLOCK

The first powerful motive that we have is our relationship to the flock. We are *overseers* of it. There are five points to remember here.

The first point to note is that the office requires us to *take heed*. What else are we overseers for? To be a bishop or a pastor is not to be set up as a demigod for the people to bow before or to live to our own carnal desires and pleasures. It is tragic when men accept a calling and do not know its true nature, so that they do not know what they have undertaken.

Consider then, brethren, where you stand and what you have taken upon yourselves! You have undertaken to be under Christ, to lead a band of His soldiers against principalities and powers and spiritual wickedness in high places. You must, then, lead them through the sharpest battles. You must learn the Enemy's strategy and battle plans. You must watch yourself and keep your hand vigilant. For if you fail, they and you, too, may perish.

You have a subtle enemy, so you must be wise. You have a vigilant enemy, so you must be watchful. You have a malicious, violent, and unwearied enemy, so you must be resolute, courageous, and unwearied. You are in a crowd of enemies, encompassed by them on every side; and so if you heed one and not all, you will quickly fall. So what a task you have before you!

See also the multitude before you. What a pitiful life it is to reason with people who have almost lost all use of their reasoning faculty. What frustration it is to talk to obstinate, willful people who know what they want but do not know why they want it. To argue with such is to talk to those who do not understand themselves—let alone you. Yet they are so confident that they are right when they have no reason other than self-confidence. Their will is the reason for their judgment and lives. Since it satisfies them, it must satisfy you.

What a world of wickedness we have, brethren, in which we contend even for one soul. And what a number of such worlds! What roots their sins have! How strange truth is to their ears! When you have done all that you can, wicked ones are at their elbows to contradict all that you have said. They will cavil and carp and slander you, so that they will disgrace your message and draw their listeners away from Christ. Your own speech to the sinners is responded to ten to twenty times by satanic messengers.

How evil, too, do the cares and business of the world devour and choke the seed that you have sown! What an abundance there is of lust, passions, and bad spirits when you leave your words with them. Even when you think you have succeeded, and you have seen people under trouble confess their sins and promise reform and have begun to be zealous converts—alas, you discover it is all false at heart and unsound after all. Superficially they have changed, but they take up with new companions and new opinions, and they still lack new hearts. How many there are who appear to have a significant change of life, but when the profits and honors of the world deceive them, they really do not stand at all.

So the second point is, consider that all this work is laid upon *you*. No one forced you to be an overseer of the church. So is it not common honesty to be true to your trust? See how many grow proud before they reach a settled knowledge. See how their immature intellects cause them to despise the very teacher from whom they have learned. See how they proudly despise the guidance and advice of those whom Christ has set up over them. See, brethren, what a field of work there is before us!

There is not a person you meet but who needs some help. Even the godly saints can soon languish if you neglect to encourage them. How easily, then, can any Christian be drawn into scandalous ways and dishonor the Gospel, if you do not take your ministry seriously? So let us be up and be doing with all our might. Difficulties must quicken us and not discourage us. If we cannot do all, let us at least do what we can. Let us be faithful ministers and not fail them or God.

Consider in the third place that it is you who have the *honor*. This should encourage your labor. What a great honor it is to be ambassadors of God, to be instruments for the conversion and salvation of men! But to strive for precedence and status, as prelates have done in the history of the church, is to forget the nature and the work of that office they contend about.

Though men strive and reach for those offices of honor, I have seldom seen men strive so furiously about being first at a poor man's cottage in order to teach him and his family the way to heaven. Or indeed, I have not seen men compete to be the first to bring a soul to Christ or to become the servant of all. It is strange that for all the plain teachings of Christ, men will not understand the nature of their office! If they did, they would strive to be the pastor of a whole county and more where there are 10,000 poor sinners needing help.

Fourth, you have very good privileges in your pastoral office to encourage you in your work. If you will not take up the work, how then should you enjoy its privileges? Then you are subsidized by other men's labors and live on the allowance of the common wealth. Either then you do the work or else cease to take the maintenance.

But you have far greater privileges than even this. Is it nothing to be educated so well when others are bred to be simply at the plow or the cot? Is it not a privilege to enjoy such learning when so much of the world lies in ignorance?

But above all, is it not such a wonderful life to be able to study and preach about Christ? Is it not so glorious to enter into His mysteries and feed upon them and daily to explore the ways of God? Others are grateful for the Lord's Day when they have a few hours leisure to do so. But we have nothing else to devote our whole attention in study and talk than the contemplation of His sacred saving truth. We can keep a continual Sabbath. Whether we be alone or with others, our business is about the other world.

How sweet then should be the pulpit, and what a delight

our conferences should be! All these and other such privileges should be reflected in the unwearied diligence that we should devote to our work.

Fifth, you are related to Christ as well as to the flock. As you are related to Christ, you are not only advanced, but you are also made *secure* by such a relationship, if you are faithful in the work to which He has called you. For you are stewards of the mysteries of God and rulers of His household. He who has entrusted you with such a work will also maintain you in it.

So, then, "it is required of a steward that a man be found faithful" (1 Cor. 4:2). Be true to Him, and never doubt that He will be true to you. Feed His flock, and He will feed you as God fed Elijah. If you are in prison, He will open doors. But then you must relieve imprisoned souls. God will give you a tongue and wisdom that no enemy can resist. Then you must use it faithfully for Him.

If you believe then that God has rescued you for Himself, then live for Him. Be unreservedly His for all He has done for you.

II. WE HAVE AN EFFICIENT CAUSE

The office we hold is itself the first motive of service. But the second motive is that we have an efficient cause. It is God by His Holy Spirit who makes us overseers of His church. That is why we need to take heed.

It is the Holy Spirit who makes men pastors of the church in three ways. First, He qualifies them for the office. Second, He directs those ordained to discern their qualifications and to know who are the fittest men for the task. Third, He directs the people and pastors to ascribe to them a particular charge. Then, and as now, it is the Holy Spirit who guides in these ways.

What an obligation, then, we have laid upon us in our call! If our commission comes from heaven, then we dare not disobey. When Paul was called by the voice of Christ, he was not disobedient to the heavenly vision. When Jesus called the disciples from their secular employment, they had to leave friends, home, trade, and everything else to follow Him. Although our call is not so immediate perhaps, or so extraordinary, yet it is from the same Spirit.

So it is no safe cause to imitate Jonah, to turn our backs upon the command of God. If we neglect our work, God has a spur to quicken us. If we overrun it, He has messengers to overtake us and bring us back and make us do it again. So it is better to do it the first time and not at the last.

III. We Have Great Dignity of Purpose

We have seen that motivation for service stems from the cause of our service as well as from the office we serve. A third motive is the object we serve. It is the *church of God* that we must oversee and feed. It is that church for which the world is much upheld and which is sanctified of the Holy Ghost, united to Christ, and declared to be His mystical body. It is that church that angels earnestly desire to look into and who attend as ministering spirits. Oh, what a charge we have undertaken! Shall we be then unfaithful? Have we the stewardship of God's own family and neglect it? Have we the conduct of those saints who live forever with God in glory, and shall we neglect them? God forbid!

Remember this when you hold back from doing painful, displeasing, and suffering duties and are tempted to delay about men's souls by dealing in things of minor importance and concern. Do you think this is an honorable way to treat Christ's bride? Are the souls of men whom God thought meet to see His face and live forever in His glory, are they not worthy of your utmost consideration and labor? Do you think so basely of the church of God, as if it deserved not the best of your care and help? How dare you say that men are not worthy of being looked after!

Remember the presence of God with His people, and then you will not be tempted to despise your office. The praises of the most High God are in the midst of them. They are sanctified, a peculiar people, a kingly priesthood, a holy nation, a choice generation—to show forth the praises of Him who has called them.

Yet dare you neglect them? What a high honor it is to be but one of them, yea, a doorkeeper in the house of the Lord. To be the priest of those priests and the ruler of these kings, such are the honors and the obligations you have. How, then, does it multiply your obligations to have diligence and fidelity in such a noble cause?

IV. WE OVERSEE THE CHURCH REDEEMED IS BY A PRECIOUS RANSOM

The final motive mentioned in my text is the price paid for the church we oversee. God the Son has purchased us with His own blood. What a motive, then, this is for those of us who need to be aroused from negligence in our work! What an argument this is to condemn those who will not be quickened to do this duty for it! Shall, then, the blood of Christ be shed in vain?

Let us then hear the words of Christ, whenever we feel the tendency growing in us to become dull and careless. "Did I die for them, and you will not look after them? Were they worthy of my blood, and yet they are not worth your labor? Did I come down from heaven to earth, to seek and to save that which was lost, and will you not go next door or to the next street or village to seek after them? Compared with Mine, how small is your labor and condescension? I debased Myself to do this, but it is your honor to be so employed. Have I done and suffered so much for their salvation, and was I willing to make you a coworker with Me, and yet you refuse that little that lies within your hands?"

So every time we look upon our congregations, let us remember vividly that they are the purchase of Christ's blood. They should be regarded accordingly.

What shame it will be at the Last Day for a negligent pastor! The blood of the Son of God will plead against him. What shame for Christ to say against him, "It is the purchase of My blood that you treated so lightly." Oh, brethren, let it urge us to do our duty, lest His blood plead us to damnation.

I have now listed the motives that I find in the text itself. There are many more that might be gathered from the rest of this exhortation of the apostle. But if the Lord will fix these few thoughts within your heart, I dare say we shall have good cause to mend our ways. When this charge is wrought within our hearts, it will occur also in our ministry. Then our congregations will have cause to thank God for it.

I know how unworthy a monitor I am for you, but a monitor you must have. It is better to hear of our sins and duty from anybody than to have none at all. But before I leave this topic, there is a little more I want to say. I have eight exhortations that I want to leave with you.

FURTHER EXHORTATIONS ABOUT HOW AND WHY WE MUST DO OUR DUTY

1. See that the work of saving grace is thoroughly wrought in your own soul

For it is a fearful thing to be an *unsanctified* professor and much more so to be an *unsanctified* preacher. Does it make you tremble to open the Bible, in case you read there the sentence of your own condemnation? When you write your sermons, little do you realize that you may be drawing up the indictments against your own soul! When you are arguing against sin, you are aggravating your own. When you proclaim to your hearers the riches of Christ and His grace, you publish your own iniquity in rejecting them and your own unhappiness in being without them.

What can you do in persuading people to come to Christ, in drawing them away from the world, and in urging them to a life of faith and holiness, when you say these things to your own confusion? If you mention hell, you mention your own inheritance. If you describe the joys of heaven, you describe your misery that you have no right to it.

What a miserable existence for anyone to have, that he should study and preach against himself and spend all his days in a cause of self-condemnation? Such a one should be the most unhappy creature on earth. Yet commonly he is the most unconscious of his own condition. He has so many counterfeits that seem like the gold of saving grace, and so many splendid stones that look like the Christian's jewel, that he seldom worries over the thoughts of his own poverty. He thinks he is rich, lacking nothing, when in reality he is poor, miserable, blind, and naked.

He is acquainted with the Holy Scripture. He is engaged in holy duties. He reproves other men's faults. He preaches for the need of holiness in heart and life. How then can such a man choose anything else but holiness? That the ordinance of God should be the occasion for our delusion is a tragedy.

How awful that we should show other men the looking glass of the Gospel to see the true state of their souls and yet never look into it ourselves! Such ones should stop short, reflect, and begin to preach to themselves before they begin to preach again to others. Otherwise, on the day of reckoning, they will say, "Lord, we have prophesied in Your Name." And they will hear the words, "Depart from me, I never knew you" (Matt. 7:23).

So I will advise such a one to take up Origen's sermon on Psalm 50:16–17. "But to the wicked, saith God, what hast thou to do to declare my statutes, and that thou shouldest take my covenant into thy mouth, seeing thou hatest instruction and hast cast my words behind thee?" When he has read this text, let him sit down and expound and apply it by his own tears. Then let him make a free confession of his sins and lament his case before the assembly and desire the earnest prayers to God for pardoning and renewing grace.

So let him come close to Christ with his heart. (Before he had only admitted Him to his brain.) Then let him preach Christ when he knows Him. In this way he may speak what he now really feels and can now commend the riches of the Gospel by his own personal experience.

Truly it is a common danger to the church to have unregenerate pastors. It is a calamity to have many men become preachers who are still not Christians. It is tragic to think they believe they are sanctified merely by the official standing as priest when they have not been sanctified by a real commitment to Jesus Christ as His disciples. Such can only worship an unknown God, preach an unknown Christ, and act before an unknown Spirit. Unknown is also his state. He is likely to be but a heartless preacher who has not the Christ and grace that he preaches in his heart.

Oh, that all our students in the university would consider this! What a poor business it is to spend all their time learning something about the works of God and have some expertise about biblical languages and yet not to know the Lord Himself. And how pointless it is not to exalt Him in their hearts or to be personally acquainted with that one redeeming work that would give them true happiness.

Instead, those who do not know Him walk in a vain show and spend their lives like dreaming men. While they are busy with their wits and tongues about an abundance of technical theological ideas and notions, they are still strangers to God and to the lives of His saints. If God ever woke them up by His saving grace, they would confess all their previous activities, employment, unsanctified studies, and dispositions as being like those of a dream world. Nothing then can be rightly known if God is not known. Nor is any study well managed—nor is it for any great purpose—when God is not studied.

We know little of the creature until it is set in relationship to God. Whoever overlooks the Alpha and the Omega will not see the beginning and the end. He who sees not Him in all, and who is the *all* of all, will see nothing at all. All creatures, as such, are but broken syllables. They signify nothing as separated from God. Where they are *actually* separated from God, they would cease to be, and the separation would be annihilation. So your study of physics and other sciences is worth little, if it be not God whom you seek after.

To see and to admire, to reverence and to adore, to love and to delight in God, appearing to us in all His works, and to peruse them for the knowledge of God—this is the true and only philosophy. This is the sanctification of your studies, when they are devoted to God. When God is the life of this all, then they are seen to have Him as their intended end and principal object.

When you have first learned God, or His will, you can address yourself cheerfully to the study of His works. If you do not see yourselves and all things as living, moving, and having their being in God, you see nothing, whatever you may think you see. For God is all in all (Rom. 11:36), and without Him you may think perhaps you know something, but you know nothing as you ought to know (1 Cor. 8:2). But it is a most high and noble part of holiness to search after, to behold, to admire, and to love the great Creator in all His works.

If then the instructors of our colleges and universities would make it their principal business to acquaint their pupils with the doctrine of life, and if they would labor to set it home upon their hearts, this, then, would be a happy means to bless souls and would result in a happy church and commonwealth. But when they read divinity like philosophers—as if it were a thing of no more moment than a lesson in music, or arithmetic, and not the doctrine of everlasting life—they destroy it and foster the church with unsanctified teachers! This is why we have so many worldlings preach of the invisible blessings and so many carnal men declare the mysteries of the Spirit.

I wish I did not need to say it. But there are so many unbelievers also preaching Christ and so many atheists speaking of the living God. If they are taught philosophy prior to or without true religion, is it any wonder that their philosophy is all or most of their religion? Deifying their own brains, they know no other God. Some, like Campanella, reduce all their theology to philosophy. Others, like Thomas Hume, make Christianity merely a delusion to write *Leviathan.* Or like Lord Herbert, they write such treatises to show the world how little they value truth.

I therefore address all of you responsible for the education of our youth. You who are schoolteachers and tutors—begin and end with the things of God. Speak daily to the hearts of your students about things that must be wrought in their hearts if they are to escape being undone. Let some challenging words come from you with the authority of God about the life to come. Do not say they are too young to understand and retain these thoughts. You little know what impressions they may have at the present.

2. Live out in grace what you preach

My second exhortation is preach to yourself the sermon that you propose before you preach it to others. When your mind is enjoying heavenly things, others will enjoy them, too. Then your prayers, praises, and doctrines will be heavenly and sweet to your people. They will feel when you have been much with God.

Conversely, when I am depressed in soul, my flock will sense my cold preaching. When I am confused, my preaching is, too. Then the prayers of others will reflect my own state of preaching. If we, therefore, feed on unwholesome food, either of errors or of fruitless controversies, then our hearers will likely fare the worse for it. Whereas if we abound in faith, love, and zeal, how it will overflow to the refreshing of our congregations and to the increase in the same graces in others!

So, brethren, watch over your own heart. Keep out sinful passions and worldly inclinations. Keep up the life of faith and love. Be much at home with God. Let it be your daily, serious business to study your own heart, to subdue corruptions, and to live dependent on God. If not, then all your work that you constantly attend to will go amiss, and you will starve your hearers. If you only have an artificial fervency, then you cannot expect attendant blessings. Above all, be much in secret prayer and meditation.

For your people's sake, then, look into your own hearts. If spiritual pride overtakes you, and you develop any dangerous ideas of schisms, and you try through your own overvalued inventions to draw away disciples after you, how you wound the Christian body! Therefore, take heed to your judgments and affections. Error and vanity insinuate slyly. Apostasies usually have small beginnings. How easily also will bad spirits creep into our affections, and our first love for the Lord cools.

A minister should take special care of his own heart before he goes before his congregation. If it is cold, how is it likely to crown the hearts of the hearers? Go then especially to God for life, and read some rousing, challenging books. Meditate on the theme and thirst for the subject that you are about to speak on. Carry the burden of your people's souls on you before you go to the house of the Lord.

3. Do God's work with all your might

I now want to stir you up to the great work of God. Do it with all your might. Speak to your people as those who must be either awakened here or in hell to their needs. Look upon your congregations hopefully and with compassion. Speak not one cold or careless word about either heaven or hell.

Whatever you do, let people see you in earnest. For you cannot break up people's hearts by jesting with them or by telling them jokes and speaking with flowery language. Men will not cast away their dearest pleasures upon a drowsy request of someone who does not seem to mean what he says.

The very tone of speech and pronouncement of the preaching is important. The best matters will not move people unless they are delivered movingly. So speak mutually and personally to your audience. The lack of such a familiar tone and expression is a great defect in most of our preaching. A man who has a monotone is like a schoolboy saying his lesson; few will be moved by what he says. Be aroused to the work of the Lord, and speak to your people as though their very lives were at stake.

Our sermons must be convincing. We must show how the light of Scripture and reason both shine brightly in the faces of the unsaved. For a sermon of mere words, which is without the convincing effect of evidence and other signs of life, is but a well-dressed carcass—no matter how well it is composed.

Preaching should provide for the experience of the reality of your communion among the saints, as well as for our communion with them. As those in the audience have understanding, wills, and affections, so we must use ours to communicate with theirs. For the great things that we have to commend to our hearers are not only well reasoned but also lie plainly before them in the Word of God. We should furnish them, therefore, with this store of evidence to silence all vain objections. We do so to encourage them to yield to the power of truth. We do so that they may see the truth is great and that it will prevail.

4. Keep up your earnest desires and expectation of success

Is your heart set on your labors? Do you not long to see conversions and the edification of your hearers? Do you not study and preach hopefully? If not, then you are not likely to see much fruit. So I have observed that God seldom blesses any man's work if his heart is not set upon success.

Let, then, all who preach for Christ and man's salvation be unsatisfied until they have the things for which they preach. When a man prepares a sermon only for his own sake and is sensitive only to how others will assess his abilities as a preacher, then I am forced to think that this man preaches only for himself. He drives on with a private trade of his own. He does not preach Christ, even when he preaches about Christ, however well he may seem to do it.

He who longs not for the success of his labors can have none of God's comfort. He is not a faithful laborer. For my part, I confess that I marvel at some aged, reverend men who have lived twenty, forty, or fifty years with an unprofitable congregation. They have seen so little fruit for their labors; it is scarcely discernible. How can they have so much patience to go on! If it were to be my situation—although I dare not leave the vineyard or quit the calling—yet I suspect I would question if it was not really God's will that I leave to go elsewhere, and allow someone else to take my place who might be more suitable for the task. Nor would I myself be so easily satisfied to spend all my days in such a manner.

5. Do well as you say it is well

Also be zealous of good works. Spare not the cost, if it promotes your Master's work. In the first place, maintain your integrity and walk without offense. Let your lives condemn sin and persuade men to do their duty. Would you have your people be more careful with their souls than you are of your own? If you would have them redeem the time, would you waste your time? If you would not have them speak frivolously, see that you speak the things that will edify. Order your own failures well, if you would have them do likewise. Do not be proud and lordly, if you would have them be lowly. There is no virtue where your own example will not do more to abate men's prejudice than humility, meekness, and self-denial. Forgive injuries and be not overcome by evil, but overcome evil with good. Do as your Lord, who when He was reviled, reviled not again.

If sinners are stubborn and strong-willed and contemptuous, then flesh and blood may persuade you to take up their weapons. You may agree you need to do so to protect yourself, as well as to maintain the public good. But that is not the way to respond. Overcome them with kindness, patience, and gentleness. Spiritual excellence is the true qualification of a saint. Christ is more imitable than a caesar. It is more a glory to be a Christian than to be a conqueror. Yes, it is better to be a man than a beast, which may often exceed us in strength.

So contend with love and not violence. Set meekness, love, and patience against force, and not force against force. Remember you are obliged to be the servants of all. Condescend to men of standing. Be not a stranger to the poor of your flock, for they are apt to take your strangeness for contempt. Speak not dogmatically or disrespectfully to anyone. Rather, be courteous to the meanest, as your equal in Christ.

The second matter concerns works of charity. Go to the poor and see what they need. Then show at once your compassion to soul and body. Buy them a catechism and some small books that are most likely to do them good. Make them promise to read them. Stretch your purse to the utmost, and do all the good you can.

Think not of becoming rich. Seek not good things for yourself or posterity. What if you impoverish yourself? Will it be loss or gain? If you believe that God is your safest treasure and that increasing investments of time and wealth in His services is having the best commerce, then show that this is true.

But mark what I say. May the Lord set it in your hearts. The person who has anything in the world so dear to him that it comes between him and Christ, such is no true Christian. A carnal heart would not believe that it is Christ who has called him. I also say that the man who does not see duty as duty and cannot spare that for Christ, he also is no true Christian. For a false heart corrupts the understanding and increases the delusions of the heart.

6. Maintain your Christian and brotherly unity and communion

[Baxter has already discussed this earlier in the chapter. So we shall be selective of his admonitions in order not to repeat what he has said.]

Ministers have need of one another. They need to improve the gifts of God in each other. For the self-sufficient are the most deficient. They are commonly proud and empty men. Some argue, "We love to live privately." To which I reply, "Why, then, do you not on the same ground stop going to church—if you so love to live privately? If you mean that you love your own ease and convenience better than God's service, then say so, and speak what is really in your minds."

Another need is the peace and unity of the church universal. So do not introduce too readily any novelties into the church. Tolerate understandable failings. Bear with one another in things that may be borne with. Do not make a creed any longer and more necessary than God has made. So do not let any man's writings or the judgment of any party be taken as a test or made the rule—though it be right.

(1) Lay not too much stress on controversial issues that have divided godly men on both sides of the matter. (2) Lay not too much stress on those controversies that are ultimately philosophical uncertainties, such as free will, predestination, the Spirit's operation of grace, etc. (3) Lay not too much stress on those controversies that are merely verbal argument. (4) Lay not too much stress on those things that are disowned or unknown to the whole church in previous generations since the Scripture was delivered to us. (5) Much less should you lay stress on matters that some ages were wholly ignorant of. (6) And least of all, you should not put much weight on any point that no one age (since the apostles) has ever received and that all ages have held a contrary opinion about.

We look then to a time when God will heal His broken churches, and this moderation will lead to the sufficiency of the Scripture being upheld. Meanwhile, we must avoid extremes in both doctrine and communion.

The extremes of doctrine are dangerous for they tend to be

characterized by three things: (1) they make new points of faith or duty; (2) they make points fundamental for salvation that are not so; and (3) they pretend that, in the prophetic and obscure passages of Scripture, they have objective evidence and greater certainty of meaning than is actually the case. Thus I have met some with such a confident rendering of the book of the Revelation (which even Calvin did not pretend to understand) that they have framed their confession of faith upon it.

The other extreme about doctrine is to avoid any originality at all. This, too, is wrong, for we need to increase our knowledge of the truth. There is still much of Scripture that is unknown to us. Our knowledge of the truth needs also to grow subjectively, and intimately so, for the manner of our personal growth. The result will be knowing the truth more soundly and clearly than ever before.

7. Do not neglect the exercise of discipline

You need to exercise discipline in your congregations. I know some of you have had discouragement in doing so. But can we make an excuse for total neglect because of that?

How sad it is when in our preaching we live with the willful omission of any known duty! Shall we continue to postpone the same, year after year—yea, for all our days? If excuses will take away the danger of this sin, will not all men find them as you did? Do you then think it is safe to live and to die in such a known sin?

If you take some people into your fellowship as incapable of discipline, they must be incapable of the sacrament of the Lord's Supper and other expressions of church communion. Then they are no church. You will end up preaching merely as they behave. If your people are not Christians, and you have no particular churches, and you are not pastors—tell us so; we shall not blame you.

We show ourselves lazy and slothful if we are not faithful to the work of Christ. I speak from personal experience. For it was laziness that kept me off my duties so long. It is indeed a troublesome and painful work to do, and it calls for self-denial because it will expose us to the displeasure of the ungodly. But do we dare to prefer our own ease and quietness and the love or peace of ungodly people before our service to Christ our Master? Can a slothful servant look for a good reward?

The neglect of discipline has a strong tendency to delude souls. It makes people think they are Christians when they are not. For if they are permitted to live with the appearance and reputation of being Christians when they are not, then their light treatment of the ordinances of God will be scandalous along with their indifference to the reality of sin. This is especially so if it appears that it is the pastors of the churches who tolerate such laxity.

We corrupt Christianity itself in the eyes of the world when we give the assumption that (1) to be Christian is merely a matter of opinion or (2) the Christian religion demands no more holiness than the false religions of the world. If, then, the holy and unholy alike are all permitted into the same sheepfold without Christ's name to differentiate them, then we defame Christ by these actions, as if He were guilty of them.

We also make good men separate themselves from our churches by our laxity of discipline when we permit the worst of men to remain uncensured. The many honest Christians will feel they have to withdraw themselves from such a church. We shall bring the wrath of God upon us for such carelessness, in a manner such as the angel of God of the church of Thyatira reproved those erring saints (Rev. 2:20).

8. Faithfully discharge, then, the great duty of personal instruction

Finally, my last exhortation is that you discharge faithfully the great duty that you have undertaken. This is to instruct everyone in your parishes by personal catechism. [This was the great purpose for the meeting of Baxter's associates at Worcester, and for which he wrote this work.] What the result of this will be, I do not know. But I have reason to hope well of it. [Actually, family prayers and Bible study marked the homes of England for the next century and a half, leaving a wonderful legacy of personal faith in the life of the nation.]

CHAPTER 7

REASONS FOR PASTORAL INSTRUCTION

It makes me leap for joy to anticipate what pastoral work, when it is well organized, can produce. Truly, my brothers, you are privileged in such a work. It could make your own consciences rejoice in it. Your parishes and even the whole nation could benefit from it. Although we need to be kept humbled when we realize that we have neglected this ministry for so long, the prospects of now doing it and their possible results should certainly be a source of much joy.

This is not the innovation of some novel approach to our duties, but the restoration of an ancient pastoral work. Unfortunately our age is so quarrelsome that regardless of the matter we focus upon, someone or other will cast stones at us and speak evil of our efforts. If they cannot stand being rebuked or contradicted, at least let us be given space in which to do what we believe is right practice. And we believe it is right to spread the knowledge of Christ among our people—by personal ministry.

There are three major reasons why this pastoral duty should be undertaken: (1) its benefits, (2) its challenge, and (3) its necessity.

I. THE BENEFITS OF PASTORAL MINISTRY

["The personal catechizing" and instructing "every one in your parishes or congregation" that Baxter advocated with great personal success in his own parish of Kidderminster may not be possible to imitate today. But much that he says is still relevant to modern pastoral visitation and the need for more personal contacts. Baxter sums up the benefits with twenty points on this issue.]

1. Personal ministry is a vital advantage for the conversion of many souls. It is necessary that you do personal ministry on a systematic basis. Merely meeting to resolve some controversial issue, or meeting infrequently, would not have the same benefits.

Personal conversion involves two things: a well-informed judgment of basic issues and the change of will that is brought about by this truth. Moreover, we have the best opportunity to imprint the truth upon the hearts of men when we can speak to each one's personal needs. If you have the compassion of Christ, you will exercise this ministry. If you are coworkers with Christ, you will not neglect the souls for whom He died.

2. Personal ministry, when it is well managed, will also build up those being established in the faith. How can you build without laying a good foundation? How can people advance in the truth when they are not first taught the essentials? The fundamental we need to lead men to is further truth.

3. Such personal teaching will make our public preaching so much better understood and regarded. When you have acquainted the people with the principles, they will better understand all that you say. They will better perceive your intent when you have prepared their hearts and minds before-

hand. So you will not lose in public service if you have been fruitful in this private ministry.

4. Personal knowledge of each other will overcome distance, ignorance of each other, and other sources of prejudice and misunderstandings. Moreover, such familiarity will tend to encourage them to open their ears to further teaching. When we have gained their personal confidence, they will be more encouraged to expose their private doubts, seek resolution, and deal freely with their pastor. But when a minister does not know his own people, he is not able to really minister to them.

5. By means of such personal ministry we come to be better acquainted with each one's spiritual state. Then we know better how to watch over them and relate to them. We will know better how to preach to them when we know their personal problems, temptations, and sufferings. Knowing their own personal needs of prayer, the pastor will also be able to pray more intelligently for their needs.

6. Likewise, we shall know better how to administer the sacraments to them, that is, whether they are fit or unfit to receive them. Some may question whether the minister has the authority to do this. Yet we shall be able now to discern their spiritual condition in a more unquestionable way.

7. We shall also be able to help our people guard against their particular temptations and avoid specific errors or heresies. When men open themselves more freely to us, we shall be able perhaps to avoid schism and other spiritual infections. As it is now, many only hear us in public, and seducers in private unsay all that we have said. If we never know this or when to help them, then the evil is determined before we are even aware of it.

8. This personal ministry will also better inform people of the true character of the pastoral office. It is all too common for many to assume that the work of the ministry is merely to preach, to baptize, to administer the Lord's Supper, and to visit the sick. Since these leave wide gaps of life, they assume their pastor is irrelevant for anything else. As there are so few who do pastoral visitation, this general but false impression of pastoral ministry tends to prevail. I have no doubt, however, that when people begin to benefit from pastoral ministry, they will have a new perspective on their pastor.

In the Protestant reaction to the auricular confession to the priest within the Roman Catholic tradition, we have commonly reacted by neglecting all personal instruction. Yet I believe our neglect of personal instruction is much more a curse than confession to the priest may ever have been. Thomas Hooker, in his book *The Soul's Preparation*, insists on the need of such personal instruction; so do other Puritan writers. If any among us think, then, that when we have preached we have done all we need to do, let us realize how much more needs to be done and not neglect it.

9. Another benefit of this ministry is to help our people understand better the nature of their relationship to their pastors. They should see us not as simply necessary for their emergency situations. They should see themselves as disciples or scholars who are being taught by their pastors through personal advice and given help for their salvation.

10. It is a lamentable state of affairs in the reformation of the church and the saving of souls to have only one or two men overseeing many thousands of people within the parish. This is the cause of much of England's misery and a reason for the spiritual famine within our cities. So alas, we see multitudes of

carnal, ignorant, sensual sinners all around us. The governors of our nation need to realize the consequences of this, for our rulers have not seen the necessity to have more than one or two ministers for each parish.

[Baxter prophetically senses something that actually took place later in the Industrial Revolution when the rapid expansion of the cities removed the working class from the benefits of church ministry. The result was that a whole sector of population arose that never had Christian nurture. The process of secularization within the cities thus continues to this day.]

11. Another benefit that is likely to follow personal ministry is the effect it will have on the next generation. Customs and habits need to be broken, and our hope in doing so lies in further generations to do so. So we work with the future in mind.

12. Likewise, to work personally with people enables us to correct false values and vanities and brings about repentance. Many an hour is lost, and many thousands of idle thoughts and words our congregation becomes guilty of, need to be personally corrected.

13. It will encourage a much better use of the Lord's Day when the head of a family has undertaken to lead his household in the proper celebration of the Lord's Day. Personal ministry promotes this.

14. Also, it will give ministers a higher priority of their duties and of their time spent. It will correct idleness, misspent time, and worldliness. For he will have to guard his time more carefully in undertaking his pastoral ministry.

15. There are also many personal benefits to the ministers themselves, including the spiritual growth of graces, peace of conscience, and personal satisfaction. It will engender heavenly-mindedness. This constant occupation with God,

with Christ, and with holiness will do much to help us overcome the flesh and its inclinations.

16. The emphasis on personal ministry will also divert our
attention away from vain controversies and from using our
care and zeal in the lesser matters of religion. These lesser matters often hinder our spiritual edification. Focus on pastoral
care will keep us from schisms and other evils.

17. This emphasis would also do much to set people right
about many controversies that now trouble the church and so
put an end to our differences. It would establish people in
sound doctrine—the mere study of it does not do this. It would
take us back to the primitive simplicity of the faith and help
us to live upon the essentials of faith. And it would help resolve many of our quarrels, which could not otherwise be
resolved.

18. The purpose of such personal ministry is the reforming
and saving of all the people in our congregations. Although
we cannot hope to affect everyone, yet our success can be more
broadly based than we had hoped. If God would have all men
to be saved and to come to the knowledge of the truth, then we
need to do likewise in our vision of ministry.

19. Such a vision is likely to bring spiritual renewal over all
the nation. What a happy thing it would be to see all England
brought before Christ and to witness a national revival.

20. Finally, so important is this need for personal ministry
that the major emphasis for the church renewal must consist of
it. It must be the major factor in making effective all our
prayers, promises, desires, and endeavors for it. How long
have we talked about the need for the reformation! How much
have we spent time in discussing it! How deeply have we
vowed to work toward its end! Yet how shamefully have we

neglected personal ministry and nurture and now seen the significance of this within the context of reformation.

The reformation has been to many of us rather like the Messiah is to the Jews. Before He came, they prayed and longed for Him, boasted of Him, and rejoiced at the hope of His coming. But when He came, they hated Him and would not believe He was indeed the Person.

Therefore they persecuted Him and put Him to death to the curse and confusion of their nation. "The Lord whom ye seek shall suddenly come to His Temple, even the Messenger of the Covenant whom ye delight in. But who can abide the day of His coming, and who shall stand when He appeareth?" (Mal. 3:1–2).

So it is with the reformation for too many. They had hoped for a reformation that would bring them more wealth and honor with the people and power to force men to do what they wanted. Now they see instead a reformation that must put them to more humility and suffering than ever they had anticipated beforehand.

This will not go down with them. How many carnal expectations are thus contradicted! Hence there are such deeply personal reactions to the reformation.

If, then, you will faithfully perform, brethren, what you have agreed upon, in catechizing, in personal instruction, and in discipline, you will do far more for the true reformation than you can ever imagine. If bishops will do this work, I will see them as reformers. If elders will do so, I will also take them to be reformers. Those who neglect and hinder it, I will only see as *deformers*.

So, dear brethren, it is you, and such as you, who under Christ must yet give this nation the fruit of saints' prayers and pains, their cost in blood and heavy sufferings. All they have been doing over many years for the good of the church and for the true reformation was but to prepare the way for you to come in to do the work that they desired to see done.

They have opened the door for you, at exceeding cost and sufferings. They have put the building instruments into your hands. Will you now stand and loiter?

God forbid!

Up, then, brethren, and give the nation the fruit of their cost and labor. In the name of God, take heed that you do not disappoint all these hopes!

II. The Difficulties of Pastoral Ministry

1. Taken on their own, the difficulties of personal ministry would be discouragements rather than motives.

But taken in the context of the benefits we have already referred to, these difficulties excite us to greater diligence. They urge us to do the work of the Lord. For in ourselves, we have much laziness and indifference.

2. We have also a base tendency to be men pleasers in our disposition of character. So we would rather men should perish than to lose their regard. We would rather they go quietly to hell than to upset them. We are ready to venture on the displeasure of God rather than to bring forth the ill will of men.

3. Some of us have a foolish bashfulness that makes us shy to speak to people plainly. We are so modest that we blush to speak for Christ, to contradict the Devil, or to save a soul. At the very same time we are less ashamed of our shameful acts.

4. We are so carnal that our fleshly interests push us to be unfaithful in the work of Christ. We are afraid of losing our

income, of bringing trouble upon ourselves, and of setting people against us. All of these require diligence to overcome.

5. The greatest impediment of all is that we are weak in the faith. How then can we help those who are also weak in the faith? Our whole motion will be weak if the mainspring within us is weak. What need, then, there is for all ministers to look well to their own faith, both within themselves and in their work! They all need to see especially that the agreement with the truth of Scripture—about joy and the torments of the life to come—is sound and lively.

6. Last, we have commonly a great deal of unskillfulness and unfitness for this work. How few know how to deal with an ignorant, worldly man for his salvation! To get within him, to win his heart and suit all personal discussion with him to his own condition and temper—this requires much skill. To choose the most suitable topics and to follow them through with the holy mixture of seriousness, terror, love, meekness, and evangelical winsomeness—this is ever so vital.

Who is fit for these things? I seriously believe it is as hard, if not harder, to confer properly with such a worldly person as it is for us to prepare our public sermons. So all of these difficulties and challenges should arouse us to draft resolutions, to make preparations, and to exercise much diligence that we are not overcome by them. Nor should we be hindered from the work of personal and pastoral ministry.

To our own congregations, we have also many difficulties to overcome.

First, too many of our people are obstinate and unwilling to be taught. They even refuse to come near us. Second, there are those willing but so extremely slow to learn. So they keep away because they are ashamed of their ignorance, unless we are wise and diligent to encourage them. Third, when they do come, so great is their ignorance that it is difficult to get them to understand. These leave as ignorant as when they first came. Further, and harder still, they may be wounded to the quick and react in hardness of heart. So if you have not seriousness, fervency, and fitness of expression, what good can you expect? When all is said and done, the Spirit of Grace must do the work.

Fifth, when you have made some desirable impressions on their hearts, unless you keep closely in touch with them, their hearts may relapse to their former hardness. They return to their old companions and temptations, effectively aborting all work.

III. THE NECESSITY FOR PASTORAL MINISTRY

We have already seen the basis of scriptural precepts for this work. For every Christian is obliged to do all he can for the salvation of others. But every minister is doubly obliged, because he is separated to the Gospel of Christ, and he has also to give himself up wholly to that work (Rom. 1:1; 1 Tim. 4:15).

Even old teachers need to be reminded of Hebrews 5:12; they, too, need to be exhorted concerning "the first principles of the oracles of God." That the unconverted need conversion and that we have the means—I trust these facts are not doubted among us. Let them who have taken the most trouble with their congregations test them. Let them see if many of their people are not still as ignorant and careless about the Gospel as if they had never heard it.

For my part, I study to speak as plainly and effectively as I can. Next to my private study, this is my first priority. Yet I frequently meet some of my hearers who have listened to me for eight or ten years and still do not know whether Christ be God or man. They wonder when I tell them of His birth, life, and death. They still do not know that infants have original sin. Nor do they know the nature of repentance, faith, or the holiness required of them. Most of them have only a vague belief in Christ, hoping that He will pardon, justify, and save them. And the world still holds their hearts.

I know that public preaching of the Gospel is the most excellent means of ministry because we speak to so many at once. Other than that single advantage, it is usually far more effective to preach the Bible's message privately to a particular sinner. In public we may not use the more homely expressions, and our speeches are so long that we overrun our hearers' understanding and memory. Thus they are not able to follow us. But in private we can take them at their own pace of understanding and keep their attention by argument, answers, and objections as they raise them. I conclude, therefore, that public preaching is not enough. You may study long but preach to little purpose unless you also have a pastoral ministry.

See from Christ's own examples how He used dialogue in preaching to His disciples and to the Jews. Note also the apostles' example. Thus Peter preached to the Jews (Acts 2), and to Cornelius and his friends (Acts 10), while Philip conversed with the eunuch (Acts 8) and Paul spoke to the jailer (Acts 16). These are a few among many other examples. Paul preached privately to them of reputation, lest he should have run and labored in vain (Gal. 2:2).

No doubt this need of pastoral ministry is included in the earliest charge that Paul gave in 2 Timothy 4:1–2. "I charge thee, therefore, before God and the Lord Jesus Christ, who shall judge the quick and the dead at His appearing, and His kingdom. Preach the word; be instant in season and out of season. Reprove, rebuke, exhort, with all long-suffering and doctrine." Both preaching and all sorts of personal reproofs and exhortations are here required.

There is also the necessity to do this duty indefinitely. First, it is necessary to bring greater glory to God by the fuller success of the Gospel. It is to the greater glory of God when we take the course that will be the more effective. So what a greater glory it would be for God if we pursued this pastoral ministry in all the parishes of our nation. If, therefore, we can increase the number and the strength of the saints, we thereby increase the honor of the King of saints. For He will have then service and praise when before He had disobedience and dishonor.

This duty is also necessary for the welfare of our people. Obviously it tends much toward their salvation. So, brethren, can you stand by and hear the Macedonian cry, "Come and help us," and refuse your help?

I must further tell you that this ministerial fidelity is necessary for your own welfare as much as for your people's sake. So if you do not care for others, at least care for yourselves.

I am afraid the day will come when unfaithful ministers will wish they had never known the pastoral charge committed to them. They will rather that they had followed other jobs than be pastors of Christ's flock! For besides their other sins, they will also have the blood of so many souls to answer for.

We, too, shall die. Die we must; there is no remedy, no wit, no learning, no credit, no popular applause that can delay the time. Willing or unwilling, our souls must go into a sphere where our persons and worldly interests will not be respected. Oh, then for a clear conscience that can say, "I live not to myself but to Christ. I spared no pains; I hid not my talent. I concealed not men's misery or the way of their recovery."

So gird up the loins of your minds, and conduct yourselves like men, that you may end up your days with Paul's triumphant confidence. "I have fought a good fight. I have kept the faith. I have finished my course. Henceforth, is laid up for me a crown of righteousness, which God, the righteous judge, shall give me" (2 Tim. 4:7).

To be coworkers with God and His Spirit is not a small honor. To be involved in the salvation of men for Christ's sake is not a light thing. So do we need to heap up a multitude of words to persuade you to a known and weighty duty? Indeed not, though many witnesses will be ready to rise up against us to our own condemnation if we do not take heed to our pastoral ministry: our parents, our teachers, our own gifts, our learning, our voluntary undertaking of the souls who trusted us, all the precepts of Scripture, all the examples of prophets and apostles, all the sermons we have preached, all the honor we expected from our ministry, all the efforts to establish the Reformation, even our own vows and promises. What if we have to say, "Great is the wrath of the Lord that is kindled against us, because we have not done according to this Covenant" (2 Kings 22:13; 2 Chron. 34:21)?

[Baxter then deals with specific objections that related to his times over some twelve pages that we do not need to repeat here.] But for all times, one thing is necessary: "Seek ye first the Kingdom of God and His righteousness" (Matt. 6:33). Again, "Necessity is laid upon us, and woe unto me, if I preach not the Gospel!" (1 Cor. 9:16) It is this that will make all our burdens light, and all our sufferings tolerable, when we have this necessity ever before us. He who knows that he serves God will never be a loser and will not need to fear whatever hazard he runs into.

So, brethren, I will not spend more words in exhorting wise merchants who already have sold all for the pearl of great price. I shall take it for granted that you are resolved to have the utmost diligence and fidelity in this work.

PART III

SOME DIRECTIONS FOR PRESERVATION OF THE FELLOWSHIP

CHAPTER 8

DIRECTIONS FOR THE EFFECTIVE MANAGEMENT OF PASTORAL WORK

We can now proceed to directions for effectively managing this work of pastoral ministry. So great is the work
that we have before us that it would be tragic if it should be
destroyed at its birth. It would be tragic for it to perish in our
hands. We have a difficult generation to deal with. And
though it is past our ability to change a carnal heart without
the effectual grace of the Holy Spirit, yet it is usual with God
to work by a means. Then He blesses the right endeavors of
His servants.

Perhaps the chief danger on our part is the lack of diligence
and skill that we may exercise. Of the former, I have spoken
much already. For the latter part, I am so well aware of my
own unskillfulness, that I wonder if I can give any directions
myself, except to the younger, inexperienced pastors. Yet I
must say something, because of my deep concern for the welfare of the church and for our nation. Both depend so much on
the management and success of our pastoral work.

There are two points you need to be concerned about. First,

you need to encourage your congregation to submit to this course of private instruction. If they will not come near, what good can they receive? Second, I am concerned that you be as effective as possible when the members of your congregation come to you for help and instruction.

I. PRACTICAL DIRECTIONS

Make sure that the minister so behaves himself in his ministry and life that his people will tend to be convinced of his ability, sincerity, and unfeigned love for them.

If his people think that he is ignorant, they will despise his teaching and think themselves to be as wise as he is.

If they think he is self-seeking or hypocritical, and one who does not mean what he says, they will suspect all that he says and does for them. They will not regard him.

If they think that his only thought is to domineer, to trouble, and to upset them, they will run away from him, as one whose efforts are viewed with disgust and hate.

But when they are convinced that he understands what he is doing and is confident in his own abilities, then they will reverence him and be docile to his teaching.

Because I am writing to those who are too modest to think they are very able and therefore despair of receiving such respect, I would say three things. First, you need to study and to work all you can. Second, you need to be as faithful as possible. This will give you the respect of those who see that you are wiser than they are. Third, what you lack in ability can be made up in other ways. Then your advice will be as effective as that of others more able.

If ministers were only content to seek the interests of their people in self-sacrificial ways, and if they became intimate, loving, and prudent in their relations, abounding in every good work, they might do so much more than they normally do. Not that we should have an interest in them from self-interest, but instead it should be only for the promotion of the interest of Christ and the furtherance of their salvation. Work, then, so that you will have gained some interest from your own people by affection and esteem, and then you will be able to lead them the more effectively.

Then what should a minister do who has lost the respect of his congregation members? If they are unworthy of him, insensitive, or those who misrepresent his zeal and good on their behalf, then he must be patient and meek, continuing to instruct them. Eventually they will be led to repentance. But if it is because of some weakness that the pastor shows in himself, or because of a difference in opinion, or merely from a personal prejudice, then let him try to remove all the prejudices he can. If he cannot do so, then let him tell them that his labors are not for himself, but for their own sakes.

If all this is to no avail, and they cannot accept his personality and ministry, then let him resign. This will allow someone else who may be more suitable to the task to be their pastor. To stay on is to frustrate his own gifts and to hold back the good that the congregation may be more open to receive from another more compatible minister.

These personal dynamics are obvious. Suppose you are happy with your congregation. The next question is, What are the most effectual means to convince them of the benefit and necessity of your personal and pastoral teaching to their souls? The way to convince anyone of what you are offering is surely to show that it is good and necessary for the individual. This requires plain and challenging sermons. Show the benefit and necessity of divine truth and of the basic principles they should grasp.

Hebrews 5:12 illustrates this well. God's oracles must be men's lessons. Ministers must teach these, and people must learn them. The oracles of God contain basic principles that all should know in order to be saved. Then it is to be expected that they will thrive on this knowledge and on its teaching. If they do not, it is because of some sickness in their lives. If any have lived long in the church without learning these basic principles of the faith, then—however old they are—they still need to start again and learn them from the beginning.

In the world, men cannot do their business without specific knowledge or learn a trade without adequate apprenticeship. Likewise, it is a contradiction for a Christian to refuse to learn the basic tenets of Christianity. If you are, then, as a Christian, a disciple of Christ, how can you refuse to be taught by Him? In the very same manner, a refusal to be taught by the minister is therefore a refusal to be taught by the Lord Himself.

Let the congregation, therefore, see that it is not merely an arbitrary matter of your own devising and imposing upon them, this matter of teaching them. Necessity is laid upon us to do so as is our calling of God. But let them see that this is profitable for their own moral improvement and growth in the reality of their salvation.

As you know, it has been the whole vision of this book, and behind that the program of our own parish, to teach the catechism—or basic tenets of the faith—to every family within the parish. Let them know that you will visit each of their homes with these instructions in mind and provide them with the necessary books that will help them. We have already celebrated a day of repentance and humiliation by the whole church. And we have taken up an offering that will defray the cost of the circulation of these works. Give them, then, a month or six weeks so that they have time to read the books on basic Christianity that you have distributed.

Be sure that you are gentle with them. Give them encouragement as much as you can. Tell them that if they would learn the basics of the Christian faith from any other book, then you will also accept that.

Accept also the reality that the older members may have poor memories and that they will not be able to learn as effectively as the younger members. Do not cut off those who are not willing to submit to the system of teaching that you have introduced. But reason with them and be patient, for charity beareth long and is kind.

II. EFFECTIVE TEACHING

Once the families begin to study the catechism, next see how you can teach them most effectively. For it is easier to compose a sermon than it is to deal with an ignorant man intimately about the necessary principles of faith. Moreover, it does not matter how many sermons you preach, if you cannot lay the foundation of basic personal instruction. Without the latter, all your labor will be in vain.

1. When you bring your home study group members together as one family or more, set them at ease and show them how much you really care for them. Show them by your own example that you have not spared any trouble; you have made this a high priority to be with them for the purpose of catechism. Take your desire to be a spiritual director seriously.

2. When you have thus spoken to them all, take the persons one by one and deal with them as far as you can in private, out of the hearing of the rest. For some of them cannot speak freely before others. Some of them cannot endure questioning before others, because they think that being embarrassed about others hearing their answers is shameful. Others again are self-conscious and will do better if they are able to discuss matters privately. You must therefore be very prudent to prevent all these embarrassments.

But the main reason for one-by-one teaching (as I find by experience) is that people will take better to plain, intimate discussions about their sins, unhappiness, and sense of consciousness in this fashion: when you talk with them privately. Be careful, however, not to create unnecessary scandal by speaking to women on their own when it would be wiser to speak in the presence of others. All these small things deserve attention because they are part of a work that is very important. Small errors may hinder a significant work for good.

3. Begin your work by taking into account what they have already learned of the catechism; receive their answers to each question. If they are able to recite little or nothing of it, try to see whether they can familiarize themselves with the Apostles' Creed or with the Ten Commandments.

4. Then choose some of the more important doctrinal questions. Ask them what they think becomes of man after death. Or what do they believe about sin? Or what is the judgment that sin deserves? Or what remedy has God provided for the saving of sinful, miserable souls? Discuss with them how they are saved by the blood of Christ.

These and other questions will enable them to focus on the realities of what repentance, faith, or forgiveness of sin are.

Ask them about regeneration and sanctification. In every case, so word your questions that they may see clearly what you mean and so that they see the answers that you expect from them. Be gentle with them. If you see there is one who does not know how to answer, take the burden from him by answering the question yourself. Do this thoroughly and plainly and make as full an explanation of the matter as you are able to.

5. When you have given them a broad survey of the fundamentals of the faith, proceed then to instruct them according to their own specific needs and character. If, for example, you are teaching a professor, then focus on what he most needs for a further explanation of the doctrines of the Gospel or the duties that he should perform. If it be someone who is very ignorant, then recite once more the whole survey of the character of the Christian faith in as few words as possible. As each one differs in ability, so speak to his specific needs.

6. It is now time to make a discerning inquiry into their own personal life. In the best and least offensive way possible, convince them of their own personal need. Remember, it is the Holy Spirit Himself who enlightens men's minds and softens their hearts and turns them from the power of Satan to God by faith in Christ, making them a sanctified, peculiar people to God. Discern and try to see if they are truly converted. See that they have a sense of assurance and of the forgiveness of sin. Ask them if they have a real sense of the enjoyment of God in their lives.

7. If you discover by your inquiries into their spiritual state that they are apparently still unconverted, then endeavor with all your skill and power to bring their heart to a sense of its condition. Show them that, as the sick require a physician, so they require Christ. Argue that if they learn to do their business in

the world, they really have no reason why, in a like manner, they have not learned to do the will of God.

So try and set all these things within their hearts earnestly. For if you do not get into their hearts, you have done little or nothing that will be suited for God.

8. I conclude this whole discussion with a practical exhortation. It consists of two parts. The first: Know that the duty of the heart is to be opened to Christ and to be contained by Christ. The second: Show externally by the avoidance of former sins and the change of life that there has been true repentance. Encourage them to change their companionship to forsake the old habits that they all once had. Do this solemnly, reminding them they are in the presence of God, who hears their promises and who will expect the performance of them.

9. Before you dismiss them, show that you are concerned that you have not offended them by your conversation. Tell them you feel as awkward in challenging them as they may feel.

Be earnest about them. Let them see that you really mean business and that nothing is more serious than their own eternal destiny and future well-being. Since you will not be able to see them often, make sure that the heads of the families do take into account their responsibilities for the spiritual control and nurture of their own household.

10. Note down in a book all you have visited in this manner. Make notes about each one: their personal responses, their own private spiritual condition, and their needs. Note those who are obstinate and who may need further discipline.

11. See also that when you are with each one, your own manners reflect the character of what you are communicating. So speak appropriately, and therefore differently, to each one.

To the dull and the obstinate, be blunt and earnest. To the tenderhearted and the fearful, be gentle, and insist on the need of their spiritual direction. To the young, lay more stress on the enticements of sensual pleasures and of the great need to have control over their passions. To the old, prepare them for death and for the need to withdraw from the foolish ways of this present world. To the young, be free; and to the old, be respectful. To the rich, preach self-denial and the deceitfulness of prosperity. To the poor, show the glory of the Gospel.

Note, too, the temptation of each age group, each sex, each profession, and each one's employment. Be as simple and humble before them as you can. Give them scriptural evidence for all that you may say. Then they will see that it is not just you, but God who is speaking to them.

Be serious in all things, but especially in the way that you apply the truth to their specific needs. There is nothing that I fear more than the careless, superficial way that some ministers do their pastoral ministry in such a lifeless and formal manner. To put a few indifferent questions to their parishioners, giving them two or three cold words of advice, and doing so without any life or feeling—this is a sure way of getting negative results from their hearers.

Avoid this by taking special care to spend time with your own hearts. Excite and strengthen your belief in the truth of God above all. For this work will test the strength of our faith. He who is only superficially a Christian, and not sound in the faith, will find his zeal flags easily. Unaffected fervency and hypocrisy will not last long in duties to be done. The pulpit is for the hypocrite a mere stage.

It is vital that we prepare ourselves for the pulpit, and therefore in private prayer. Show clearly your loving concerns for your people's souls. In private discussions with them, show that you give them nothing else but their salvation.

If you are limited with time, take several together. This is much better than to be hasty with individuals and superficial in your contacts with them. Be sure those you bring together are common friends so that they will hold each other's confidences while you talk with them.

Lastly, if God enables you, extend your charity to the poorest of people. Give them a contribution toward their relief, and compensate them for the time that is taken off their work while you are instructing them. I know that you cannot give what you do not have. But speak to those who can help with this matter.

As for those who are under the fear and depression, I shall not deal with them now. I intend to focus this discussion on a different purpose. I have already as much as I think is necessary in my published work entitled *Directions for Peace of Conscience.*

CHAPTER 9

SOME DIFFICULTIES IN PASTORAL TEACHING

It is likely that you will meet some awkward people who will create difficulties during your ministry. There will be the opinionated questioners, prompted by conceit and pride. They are readier to teach than to be taught. They may argue with you as if you were ignorant and needing instruction yourself. If they are also cantankerous, they will waste your time with foolish arguments and much dispute rather than seek to learn anything.

It is also likely you will have some who come to you and accuse you of belonging to a false church because of your bad members. They will challenge how you administer the sacraments, how your denominational administration operates, what scriptural evidence you have for praying or singing psalms in a mixed audience, and much else.

If you meet such people, let them know that your pastoral ministry for catechism is not the proper place to discuss these aforementioned matters. Let them know that you are not trying to avoid their challenges and questions. You will entertain them on a more suitable occasion.

Ask the questioner to first of all concentrate on the catechism and recognize that this is the proper purpose of this particular meeting. It is also more important to focus on the fundamentals of the faith than the detailed scruples that some-one wants to argue over. If he accepts this, then concentrate on the essentials of the faith with him, especially within the context of Scripture. For it is more likely that you will find he is very ignorant of the biblical fundamentals.

Be very careful with him if he is a perversely schismatic individual or a heretic who is dogmatic in his views and filled with pride. If so, you may have little hope for his recovery. But if you find him to be godly and temperate, then you may hold out much hope for him. Do not disparage him or let bitter words be spoken. This is essential, since we need to be tender to the reputation of all good men. We must bear one another's burdens and not add to them. We must restore those with a spirit of meekness, who may fall through weakness, remembering we, too, may also be tempted. Remember, also, that it is unlikely you will help those you have exasperated and turned against you.

See to it that those very persons, for whom you have some hopes, are treated in tenderness and love. For when they have been badly dealt with, they can become as selfish, proud, and even more impatient of reproof than many of the more secular-minded people.

At the conclusion of your meeting, if you find yourself with those who dispute and enter into controversy and debate, tell them this: You would rather learn than dispute. When you have heard all they have to say, make it clear it is not new to you. If you are given divine evidence for it, then you have received it long ago. If it is contrary to the truth, then you would rather have the truth. If they desire to learn of your evidence, tell them. Challenge them to study the evidence of the faith itself. If they refuse, then they can only prove to be unfaithful to the truth.

When you part with such, be sure that you try to sum up the truth about which you do agree. If the differences are not fundamental, then discuss that. If the differences are small, then warn such of schism and of the sad ways in which the work of the Lord can be held back by such minor differences. I speak, of course, only of the personal differences that we may disagree about and not on serious matters of heresy and major error.

[Here Baxter cites a sermon that Bishop Ussher preached before the king, James 1, on church unity. It commented on what a tragedy it is that while there is disunity between Roman Catholics and Puritans, the masses remain religiously illiterate. This results from their being neglected in the dissensions and jealousies.]

How to Deal with Schismatics

Having advised you what to do with such men when they appear for private instruction, consider how you should behave toward them on other occasions. In the preservation of peace and unity for your congregation, much may depend on your right handling of such people. Alas, all too often those people who divide us in the church are commonly those who profess more than ordinary religious zeal.

1. Your first responsibility is to preserve the church from such people. For it is more than likely that if you try to correct them of their false ways, they will only turn to some other error. They seldom recover true faith. Like a bee flying from one flower to the next, they go from one source of error to another.

2. Normally the minister should have more knowledge and

ability in spiritual matters than his congregation. He should be able to teach them boldly and from a position of strength.

When a proud seducer has a clever tongue and a minister is dull and ignorant, the minister can be baffled and brought into contempt. This only stumbles the weak. So when a minister can expose such, he greatly helps to preserve the church from their influence.

3. Frequently emphasize to your people the nature, necessity, and daily use of the great, unquestionable, and fundamental principles of Christianity. Let them realize that it is the main principles of faith on which life or death hangs. It does not hang on those trivial points around which controversy is so often focused.

4. Make them sensitive to the mischiefs of schism. Teach them to realize the great and certain obligations that lie upon us all to maintain the church's unity and peace.

5. When a fire is kindled, try to stamp it out from its inception. Do not even allow the smallest spark to blaze before you snuff it out. So go at once to all persons you suspect of being infected. Counsel with them until you are sure that they have recovered from their bad spirit.

6. It may be permissible to redirect a major controversial issue by raising another one that you can better control, the second not being as likely to divide the church as the first. Let them see that there are far greater difficulties than their own to be resolved. In this way they may be humbled by the awareness of their own ignorance and self-conceit.

7. Be careful that you do not always nurture your people with milk when they should be fed on stronger food. For they will then tend to be puffed up with pride. To put it another way, if they are continually hearing the same things from their

minister that they already know, they will think themselves equal or indeed wiser than you are.

Even if you do not overlook the great, fundamental truths or neglect the poor or ignorant in the congregation, you may still include a part in your sermon that will overwhelm the self-conceited and humble them. They must learn to see that they are only children and that you are able to preach much more deeply than they are capable of fully absorbing.

8. See that you do not preach against them from the pulpit. It is wise not to name them specifically or talk down about their own sect. For generally such people will be sensitive, proud, passionate, and rash. They will hate and fly upon you as an enemy and accuse you of unchristian railing. So instead of naming them, state clearly those truths that fully refute the errors they are teaching. If you do your work effectively, the error will collapse under its own weight.

When you must deal with them directly, do not do it by short, unsatisfactory applications, or much less by irritating reproaches. Rather, take up the issue without naming it specifically, state it without bias, handle it thoroughly and mildly, yet also with conviction. Give the fullest evidence from the Scriptures. But do not say all that could be said; rather, choose that which is the least likely to appear controversial.

9. Be sure to keep up your private family meetings, for these will enable you to draw them into the fellowship where you can manage them more prudently. In this way, you will be able to keep them from dividing among themselves, for here they are at liberty to say what they please without control.

In this type of meeting, be sure that you are always there yourself. Do not let contention occur. So do not let the meeting be used so that particular individuals can seek their own glory, but let it edify the people. Let all who are present know that they may ask anything that is still a doubt in their minds. Resolve the doubts yourself.

If you see some displaying their own knowledge and abilities that may possibly divide the people, mildly rebuke them. For it is for their good that you do such things. Let them know that it is a sign of a proud heart to teach when there is an appointed teacher present.

10. At the same time, try to use all the abilities of your people as much as you can. Use them as helpers in your ministry in an orderly way and under your direction. Otherwise, you may find them working in a disorderly manner and in opposition to you. It is not uncommon for schisms to develop when a minister despises contemptuously the preaching of laymen, being unwilling to use the gifts that God has bestowed on such men to assist the church.

Some ministers thrust their talented people away as if they were profane. When no hands but the minister's hands are employed in the work of the church, the work is apt to go poorly. For God does not give men gifts in order for them to be buried, but they are for the common use of the church.

Here are some of the ways that you can make best use of the abilities of your members.

(1) Urge them to be diligent in teaching and praying for their own families. (2) Urge them to step out and visit their poor, ignorant neighbors. (3) Urge them to go often to the impenitent and scandalous sinners around them, to deal with them in all possible skill and earnestness. Let them do so lovingly and patiently, in order to convert, reform, and serve their souls. (4) Acquaint them with their duty to watch over each other in brotherly love. (5) At your private meetings, or in days of

humiliation, or in private thanksgiving, employ them in prayer. (6) The appointment of deacons will help you maintain the unity of the church and the exercise of discipline, as well as give them recognition of their own usefulness.

11. With those who cause trouble and are divisive, maintain Christian love and fellowship. Maintain love even when they have begun to be warped and defective. Do not lose your interest in them, as long as you think you may be able to help them recover.

12. If they do withdraw from their own private meetings, follow them and be among them continually—as long as you can. Mildly rebuke the unlawfulness of what they are doing, but assure them that you are willing to hear what they have to say. A very common cause of schism in this country is for ministers to condemn them, or withdraw from their private meetings, or talk behind their back in condemnation of them, or even reprove them from the pulpit. It is easier to do this than to play the role of a skillful physician who seeks to cure his patient.

13. If all of these efforts do not succeed, then call in the ablest neighboring minister whom you know. Ask him to come over and help you privately.

14. Do not let the authors of schism outdo you in anything that is good. Truth should be more effectual for sanctification than error. But if you give schism workers the advantage of appearing to be more obedient to the truth than you are, they have won the day. All your further disputation will mean very little. For many will judge only by the outward appearance and the effects, unable in many cases to judge of the doctrine itself. They may think the one judged the best man will also have the best cause.

When, then, a libertine preaches free grace, you must preach it the more effectually. If he magnifies the grace of love, be all for living in pure love to God. Do not contradict him in the positive aspects, but only in the negative and destructive aspects of his teachings. So outdo him, and preach upon the love of God with its causes and motives more fully and effectually than he can with his defective teaching. This is the most effective way of settling your people against the seduction of false teaching. Remember, too, that preaching truth is the most successful way of confusing error.

Be loath also to let the dividers outdo you in the practice of a righteous and holy life, any more than you let them outdo you in sound, diligent teaching. Let us be lovers of all, and especially of all saints. Do good to all as we have power. Let us be more just than they, more merciful, humbler, meeker, and more patient. "For this is the will of God that by well-doing we may put to silence the ignorance of foolish men" (1 Peter 2:15).

Let us excel them in a holy, harmless, righteous, merciful, fruitful, heavenly life—as we do in soundness of doctrine. By our fruits let us be known. Then the weaker brethren may see the truth in our lives when they have not the insight to see it in the doctrine itself. Let our light then "so shine before men that they may see our good works, and glorify our Father Who is in heaven" (Matt. 5:16).

How happy would the church have been if, instead of all our chiding over errors and schisms, the ministers of the Gospel had taken this course. It would have had far more power.

The Lukewarm and Unsteady Christian

We have now considered three types of person with whom we are confronted. These are: (1) the ignorant and unconverted; (2) the doubting, troubled believers; and (3) the carping opinionist or seducing schismatic.

There is also a fourth kind of person who will present us as ministers with a great challenge. It is those who may have had true repentance and faith, but who remain ignorant, lukewarm, unnoted for any special profession of godliness, or perhaps inconsistent in their walk. Such causes us to be more fearful than hopeful for them.

So we oscillate between hope and fear for them, even though we cannot accuse them of being unconverted, impenitent, and unsanctified persons. I think about half of those who come to me are of this sort. Of those, I shall only briefly say the following points.

1. The first direction we have about them is tell them plainly (or bluntly): "Your case is sad. I wonder that you dare risk your salvation as you do." You may then proceed to call for some degree of confidence or give a severe censure. You should choose what you deem is good to awaken them to their actual and true state.

2. Be very cautious about passing hasty or absolute censure on any of these. For it is no easy matter to discern someone who is wholly destitute of real faith from one who professes himself to be a Christian. Some may think it is easy to do this, but it is not so. You may do your necessary counsel, then, with such people, but do not make a premature and absolute judgment about them.

3. Your general duties as a minister will provide other ways

to deal with such people. I shall only add this: (1) Keep them close to both public worship and to private devotion, such as attendance at church services, the reading of the Bible, etc. (2) Spend time often with the lukewarm to awaken them, and be with the careless in order to admonish them. (3) If they become sick, seize the opportunity to see how their hearts may be softened and their ears opened.

(4) See that they spend the Lord's Day as they ought, and watch that they manage their families aright. (5) Keep them away from temptations and other occasions of sin. (6) Urge them to keep in touch with you when they are being tempted or need your help in other straits or dangers. (7) Strike out at the great radical sins: self-seeking, earthly-mindedness, sensuality, pride, and infidelity. Help them to develop the habit of reading the Bible, and direct them to good books that will help them most. (8) Encourage their godly neighbors to keep an eye on them. (9) Keep up discipline, to make them afraid of potential scandal. (10) Maintain the life of grace in yourselves so that it may appear in all the sermons that you preach. In that way all who come cold to the church may be warmed and quickened when they leave.

I have finished my advice to you. I now leave it for you to put into practice. Although the proud may receive it scornfully, and the selfish and slothful do so with distaste and indignation, I doubt not that God will use it. For it is written, in spite of Satan's opposition, to awaken many of God's servants to their duty. And it is written to promote the work of a true Reformation. Amen.

December 25, 1655

APPENDIXES

LETTERS, AGREEMENTS, AND OBJECTIONS

LETTERS, AGREEMENTS, AND OBJECTIONS

Sometime in the spring of 1652, a monthly meeting of local ministers was held in Richard Baxter's home. At that meeting, Baxter proposed that they should adopt a common basis for church discipline. He prepared an agreement that was later accepted by less than half of the 112 parishes of Worcestershire.

The plan was widely taken up and adopted by similar associations in some thirteen other counties. This occurred in the transitional political life under the Commonwealth when some breakdown of the diocesan machinery had occurred. Baxter had great hopes of these experiments as a means of promoting the efficiency of the ministry. He saw them as a step forward to the church unity that he longed to see.

I. LETTERS OF APPEAL

In the first edition of his book, Baxter included two letters that related to a proposal he had made. He had written *The Reformed Pastor* to aid "the propagation of the Gospel and the saving of men's souls."

Now he added another concern. Writing to concerned pastors and gentlemen living in London from various counties, he said: "You know, I doubt not, the great inequality in ministerial abilities, and that many places have ministers who are not qualified with convincing concern and awakened gifts. Some must be tolerated in the necessity of the church, although they will have little impact upon worldly and ignorant people. And others, though they are learned, able men, may be unfitted to deal with simple folk.... I suppose if you peruse the whole ministry of a county, you will not find so many lively, convincing preachers as we could wish to have."

Why not, suggested Baxter, select four men in each county? Each could delegate his duties once a month to someone else and be freed to preach in the places that might most need them.

Baxter had proposed this in London, and some friends in Worcestershire had taken up the idea, providing the money needed for doing so. This encouraged Baxter to write a wide appeal in London to other merchants, landed gentry, and ministers that they do the same for other counties.

In a second letter to all the ministers of the county of Worcestershire (not within his association), he tells them of the scheme now financially supported from London and urges them to open their churches to the possible ministry of these four men appointed in Worcestershire.

"So we do hereby request of you as brethren, that when any of them shall offer their labors for your congregation, in preaching ... you will receive them, and do all in your power to further them in their work. For as we have no thoughts of thrusting their help upon you without your consent, so we cannot but undoubtedly expect that you, being men fearing God and desiring their people's everlasting good, will cheerfully and gratefully entertain such assistance. And we hope that none will think it needless, or take it as accusing the ministry of insufficiency, for the Lord does variously bestow His gifts."

Since in fact Baxter had urged his financial supporters to give to the cause of the uneven standard of ministry, we do not know how far his fellow ministers felt threatened by his scheme. Nor indeed do we know how successful the associations were at that time.

II. The Agreement of the Worcestershire Association

This agreement was published in 1653 as *The Christian Concord*, three years before *Watch Your Walk*. It contained twenty propositions, a summary of whose major points is here reprinted.

We, ministers of the Gospel ... do agree and resolve as follows:

1. Not to addict or engage ourselves to any party or set up the dictates of any party. Instead, we unanimously want only to practice those known truths that the sober and godly of such party are agreed upon. This, we trust, will give no occasion for any such sober and godly persons to be divided from us.

2. We agree and resolve by God's help to do what God makes known to be our duty. We will faithfully discharge it. This we will do even if it costs us any fears of loss in our present states, or the frowns and displeasures of men, or any similar carnal inducement.

3. Particularly, we are convinced it is the duty of every minister to try to know personally, if at all possible, all in his

charge. If he is thus acquainted with his people, he will know his special duty to each one and perform the same.

4. We are also convinced it is the duty of ministers and people, as occasion may arise, to admonish and reprove those who live in any known sin through willfulness or negligence. This must be done in tender love and yet with great seriousness and discretion, and not with malice, bitterness, and disdain. It must be suited to the needs and character of each person and offense.

5. If the offender hears not, nor obeys the admonition by repentance and reform, then he must be admonished before witnesses. This we pledge ourselves faithfully to practice according to our opportunity. And we will let our people be acquainted of their duty in this respect. This becomes extremely important in our large congregations where, because of the greatness of other works, fewer of these personal admonitions can be expected of the ministers themselves.

6. If any after the admonition still refuse to reform and to repent, then those who can prove it must tell the church officers. The officers must hear the case and admonish the offender with authority. We caution here: If private persons accuse them in public before the officers have heard the case, this may breed dangerous slanders and quarrels. We appoint certain times for the hearing of such cases.

7. In places that have magistrates we judge it convenient, if we can persuade them, to be present with us at these meetings. This way they can both witness our proceedings and countenance them as far by the law as they may.

8. If any still refuse to repent and to reform, or if any have sinned seriously so as to bring public scandal upon the church,

then it is the duty of ministers to rebuke them before all the church and to call them publicly to repentance.

9. Yet where any man's sin exposes him to the law of the land, we resolve not to anticipate public justice. Nor will we call out such to accuse themselves by their confessions in church. Instead we will wait to see what justice will do unto them. But after civil sentence, we may and must require open repentance.

10. We resolve not to mention any man's sin publicly before we have full proof of the case.

11. If after public admonition the sinner shall obstinately refuse to show repentance or reform, it is the duty of the minister to make known to him the threat with which Christ Himself denounced such willful sin, speaking in the name of Christ. He is to refrain from taking Communion. The church is to be charged, in Christ's name, to avoid all familiarity with him—not only in God's worship, but in ordinary conversation, other than that which mutual and civil relations oblige.

12. It is unsuitable to admit such a man to public communion of the Lord's Supper while he is under just trial.

13. We must also proceed to reprove such a one publicly in order to avoid stumbling the weak, offending the godly, creating a scandal to our profession, and making an offense to God.

14. It must not be a slight, unwilling, or mere verbal repentance that must satisfy the church of restitution.

15. Now if, after one or two occurrences of scandalous or obstinate sinning, a man does profess serious repentance, we shall admit him to communion.

16. Although the people do not have ministerial or governing power, yet they are to have the judgment of discretion. With it they may thereby try and discern each case.

17. If people will not avoid fellowship and familiarity with those who have been publicly judged and cast out, they are to be admonished. But if a large section of the church does this, then the rest are to refrain from having communion with them. We agree that to avoid such serious and dangerous consequences, if such be the case, it is advisable to meet our brethren of that Association and to hear their judgments.

18. It has been the custom for the church since the apostolic days to have many offices. Now the personal role of the ministerial duty is often very great. So we judge it lawful to use all the assistance that we can and to procure both more ministers and elders as the church may need them.

We judge it fit to utilize those members who are educated and competent to teach in private instruction and in oversight. But we do not determine as an association whether they can administer the sacrament or whether they are to be equated with teaching elders. We simply agree in practice to leave the specific status and role to the judgments of their congregations. We also think it advisable to ordain suitable men as deacons.

19. Because all of these rules of discipline cannot be exercised without the people's consent, they should be adopted accordingly. So we think it is necessary they should consent to the rules of this association and not leave it only to the minister's consent.

20. To obtain this consent, and knowing our people may be ignorant of the fundamentals of the Christian faith, we shall first instruct our people in various sermons about the nature of the church, its constitution and government, the duties and authority of pastors, and the duties of the people of God. We shall seek to be guided by God to draw up an agreed-upon confession publicly. A copy of it will be available for our peo-

ple to read and to reflect upon. Only then shall we call upon their consent.

Following this agreement the association agreed to meet in five places in the county, once a month or more often if need required. Each minister could choose which of the five places (namely, Worcester, Evesham, Upton, Kidderminster, and Bromsgrove) suited him better to attend.

A public lecture was to be given on these occasions for their edification. Matters of discipline and worship would be discussed. Any new points of doctrine should then be debated, as well as differences of opinion. Complaints should be received against any member of the association, and matters of discipline would be discussed.

Any help required of neighboring churches should be raised. Those of neighboring counties with no association should be admitted. Before resignation from the association, all reasons for doing so should be brought up. Resolve was also made not to exceed the bounds of their calling in meddling with civil or state affairs.

The purpose, then, of the association should be for the welfare of souls; the propagation of the Gospel; the unity, peace, and reformation of the church; and to glorify and please God in all.

III. OBJECTIONS TO BAXTER'S WATCH YOUR WALK

This appendix, which is added in Baxter's later editions, indicates his own reactions and insights to the criticisms that he received from the first edition of his book. He was encouraged when he says, "I bless God that I have lived to hear of so many faithful servants of Christ following closely to this work of

Personal Instruction, not only in this county, but in other parts of the land. Now I begin to hope that the pastoral office will be understood by such experience, both by our people and by ourselves.... I hope now that misunderstandings between people and their teachers will be removed. I hope they will perceive what we aim at, and how far we are from intending them any hurt, or of lording it over them. For we want them to see that our greatness and dignity simply consist in *being servants of all.*

"Next to *unskillfulness,* the greatest thing I fear in ministers is *laziness.* Lest we begin to favor ourselves ... and let flesh pervert our reason and make us say, 'I do not think it is necessary to bestir myself so hard ... I have done enough already, why do I need to do more ... ?' Most of the objections I have heard since publishing this book are the same as those answered in the preface" [chap. 1]. [But there were twenty new objections raised by the first edition, and some of these Baxter deals with in the following manner.]

Objection 1: It is objected that my whole book is based on a false supposition, namely, that discipline and personal instruction are essential to our ministry.

I did not say this, says Baxter, "but these words I did write indeed: *Ruling is as essential a part of the pastor's office as preaching, I am sure.* I conclude: (1) that it is essential to the office or ministry of a pastor of a particular church to have the power of ruling as of public preaching and to be obliged on fit occasions to rule as well as preach. (2) Actually, to rule is not essential to being a pastor. For to be a pastor is to be empowered or obliged. (3) Ruling relates to his ministerial office, as a doctor's ability to advise and counsel patients relates to his position. (4) A man may be a faithful minister and yet never preach a sermon. If a large congregation has six or more pastors, and two or three of them are the ablest preachers, the others may more wisely use their energies for discourse and private oversight."

Objection 2: We do not take the parish to be our church, but distinguish between the members of our flock, the church, and the rest of the parish.

If they take all the parish to be their church, cannot they agree to catechize and instruct them personally, because we do not take all of our parishes to be church members? They may as well also give up preaching for the same reason. We only exclude from our teaching those who have withdrawn from our charge and from a particular church, by refusing to be members of that particular church.

Objection 3: Others object when we judge obstinate despisers of instruction and find them unfit for communion.

How else can we do our ministry faithfully? Who would not condemn a physician who made his patients believe they were in no danger, in order to save himself the trouble of looking after them? It is intimidation, perhaps, that they resent most. But we cannot tolerate slackness of life within the church without making the garden of the Lord into a wilderness.

Objection 4: You cast your shoe too narrow for our foot. You judge all our congregations by your own. We happen to have stubborn people who are not so tractable as yours are, perhaps.

The fact is that the worse people are, the more they really need instruction. Can people be fit for communion who are fettered by ill-discipline? It is a contradiction.

Objection 5: But you build too much on the text Acts 20:20. The apostles taught from "house to house" simply because they had no churches.

Yes, it is true the apostolic ministry was very limited, teaching in the synagogues, in house churches, and to the mixed concourses of pagans and Christians. But I base my concern on the general duty that to be a pastor or shepherd, one is a shepherd—just as being a master, teacher, physician, or military commander means one undertakes appropriate roles to the office concerned. True, one has no authority to prescribe specifically two days a week of such pastoral instruction. But one's time commitment to it is only an indication of the seriousness with which one takes one's pastoral duties.

Objection 6: If all ministers took two days a week for pastoral ministry, they would have little time to study, and so their adversaries would find them unskilled in apologetics.

After so many years of university training, is not four days a week ample time for your study? And do you study at all? He shall be the ablest physician, theologian, or lawyer who adds practice and experience proportionate to his studies.

Objection 7: In the time in which Paul lived, more diligence was required than ours. The churches were just being planted, the enemies were numerous, and the persecution was great. But now time has changed.

This was the bishops' answer against the Puritans' insistence on the importance of preaching. But it savors of a man who is locked up in his study and is unacquainted with the world outside it.

Good Lord! Are there not such multitudes around us who do not know whether Christ be God or man, what He has done for them, and what they must trust for pardon and salvation? Are there not so many thousands all around us who are drowning in presumption, security, and sensuality, breaking the hearts of preachers, and neither feeling us nor understanding us when we have done all we can?

What conscientious minister finds not work enough to do from one end of the year to another? If he has not a hundred souls to care for, is it not still so?

Objection 8: You have determined too confidently what assistance is required for the minister's duties in a large congregation. It leaves a low financial allowance for him.

Must I turn to my Bible to show you that a man's soul is worth more than the world, and so much more than a minister's stipend? Must not every Christian ask first, In what ways can I most honor God?

Objections 9–19 deal more specifically with practices connected with the associations and are therefore not so relevant for us today.

The last objection that Baxter touched on concerned the issue of the Apostles' Creed. He replied that the use of "the ancient estern creed" indicates the church has had several creeds, eastern and western, ancient and modern. His defense of the Apostles' Creed was as follows:

A creed is a living reality and not a dead orthodoxy of static words. So I cannot believe that the present form of words now in our hands was either composed by the apostles or was the Universal Creed from the beginning. The Fathers expressed the creed of the church in various forms, so that even 300 years after Christ, differing forms of the creed existed. Ignatius, Irenaeus, Origen, and Tertullian recite at least three different forms of it.

Quoting extensively from Bishop Ussher's "Sermon of Church Unity," Baxter notes that:

This creed was the same in *substance*, yet its *form* was somewhat different, and in some places raised more enlargement than in others. I think most of us love our carnal ease so well, that if you knew where the book or the church were that would give us such a *certain* exposition of Scriptures (as from the apostles direct), we would excitedly embrace it. [Like the Koran] we would use it not only to quiet our minds, but also to spare the time and effort we now bestow on our studying of it.

INDEXES

SCRIPTURE AND SUBJECT

SCRIPTURE INDEX

SUBJECT INDEX

READERS' GUIDE

FOR PERSONAL REFLECTION OR
GROUP DISCUSSION

READERS' GUIDE
INTRODUCTION

The Victor Classic series is committed to making accessible to today's readers the powerful Christian voices of past eras. And our hope is that as you read through this book, you will use the discussion points in the following pages to take you to an even deeper level of faith through personal challenge and application.

You can study these points on your own or in the context of a group study or course work for a class. Perhaps you will even invite a friend or a group of friends to work through the book with you. Our prayer is that you will let yourself be challenged to change the way you live based on the answers you discover to life's most pressing questions.

READERS' GUIDE

Introduction

1. Richard Halverson points out that Richard Baxter lived in an era of "almost unbelievable deviation." However, the church was preserved through that time. What challenges confront the church today? What is your prognosis for its health? Defend your prognosis.

2. What three top priorities do you believe a pastor today ought to embrace? How might a congregation help its pastor keep those priorities?

Chapter One

1. What shortcomings does Richard Baxter address in this chapter? How might a pastor today be guilty of similar shortcomings?

2. What warnings does Baxter issue to laypeople? Do you believe similar warnings should be issued today? Why or why not?

3. Baxter contended that no church should be bigger than a pastor can personally supervise. What do you think a congregation's maximum size is before one pastor can no longer personally supervise it? Why did you choose that number?

Chapter Two

1. Compile a list of pastoral duties. How much time per week do you think a pastor should assign to each one? How did you decide where to assign the greatest amounts of time?

2. Which quality would you rather see in a pastor: deep humility or high intelligence? Why?

3. Jerome wrote: "When you are teaching in the church, do not let the people be excited with a shout, but let them grow. For the tears of your hearers will tend toward true praise" (p. 51). Do you believe this counsel is appropriate today? Why or why not?

4. Baxter taught that pastors ought to have patience. Do you think a pastor needs to be more patient with circumstances or people? Explain.

Chapter Three

1. This chapter admonishes pastors to practice what they preach—
   to embrace the salvation they preach to others and to avoid the
   sins they preach against. What is your opinion of preaching in
   which a pastor often discloses his personal failures in battling sin?
   Does such preaching make listeners more comfortable with their
   failures? More convinced that holiness lies beyond their reach?
   Explain your answers.

2. Why should a pastor oversee himself?

3. What considerations might tempt a pastor to be motivated by
   self-interest?

Chapter Four

1. Richard Baxter observed that the name "Puritan" became a nickname for all who "spoke seriously of heaven, of death, of judgment, and who devoted the Lord's Day to such issues." What moral and spiritual attitudes and actions today are often dubbed "puritanical"? Describe an occasion when you were called "puritanical." How did you feel? How did you respond?

2. Pride can become an insidious and subtle sin in the heart and life of a pastor. How can a congregation treat its pastor with respect and speak highly of him without causing him to become proud? Is it possible for a pastor to rebuke believers without discouraging or alienating them? If so, how?

Chapter Five

1. How well does the belief that a pastor must be a good administrator fit Baxter's pastoral model? How can a pastor minister effectively to every age level: seniors, middle-aged adults, families, young marrieds, singles, youth, and children?

2. What counseling role should a pastor fill? Should counseling be a required seminary course? Why or why not?

3. How might a pastor lead his flock in the effective practice of church discipline? Do you see a need for discipline in today's churches? Explain.

Chapter Six

1. Addressing pastors, Richard Baxter commented: "You have very good privileges in your pastoral office to encourage you in your work" (p. 130). What privileges do you associate with pastoral ministry?

2. If you could counsel a discouraged pastor, what would you say?

3. A pastor might be distracted from the main goal of ministry to invest time in secondary causes. What do you see as secondary causes a pastor ought to keep secondary?

Chapter Seven

1. What do you see as the three most rewarding benefits of pastoral ministry? Why are they so rewarding?

2. What do you see as the three biggest challenges pastors face today? Why are they such big challenges?

3. Why do you agree or disagree with Baxter's statement, "He who knows that he serves God will never be a loser" (p. 161-162)?

Chapter Eight

1. Richard Baxter wrote that a pastor should resign if he has lost the respect of his congregation and has failed to regain it (p. 167). Do you concur with his advice? Why or why not?

2. Baxter encouraged pastors to practice one-on-one teaching (p. 170). What benefits do you see in this kind of discipleship? How might a pastor promote similar discipleship among members of the congregation?

3. According to Baxter, a pastor should teach and apply the fundamentals of the faith. Do you believe churches need more or less doctrinal preaching today? Defend your answer. Do you believe biblical illiteracy is widespread in today's churches? If so, what will it take to correct this situation?

WATCH YOUR WALK

Chapter Nine

1. Baxter's advice for putting out fires in the church is to do so immediately. How might your church best extinguish each of the following fires: a fire set by gossip, a fire set by false doctrine, a fire set by immorality, a fire set by false accusers, and a fire set by disgruntled members?

2. How can a pastor deal effectively with lukewarm church members?

220

The Word at Work Around the World

A vital part of Cook Communications Ministries is our international outreach, Cook Communications Ministries International (CCMI). Your purchase of this book, and of other books and Christian-growth products from Cook, enables CCMI to provide Bibles and Christian literature to people in more than 150 languages in 65 countries.

Cook Communications Ministries is a not-for-profit, self-supporting organization. Revenues from sales of our books, Bible curricula, and other church and home products not only fund our U.S. ministry, but also fund our CCMI ministry around the world. One hundred percent of donations to CCMI go to our international literature programs.

CCMI reaches out internationally in three ways:

· Our premier International Christian Publishing Institute (ICPI) trains leaders from nationally led publishing houses around the world.

· We provide literature for pastors, evangelists, and Christian workers in their national language.

· We reach people at risk—refugees, AIDS victims, street children, and famine victims—with God's Word.

Word Power, God's Power

Faith Kidz, RiverOak, Honor, Life Journey, Victor, NexGen — every time you purchase a book produced by Cook Communications Ministries, you not only meet a vital personal need in your life or in the life of someone you love, but you're also a part of ministering to José in Colombia, Humberto in Chile, Gousa in India, or Lidiane in Brazil. You help make it possible for a pastor in China, a child in Peru, or a mother in West Africa to enjoy a life-changing book. And because you helped, children and adults around the world are learning God's Word and walking in his ways.

Thank you for your partnership in helping to disciple the world. May God bless you with the power of his Word in your life.

For more information about our
international ministries, visit www.ccmi.org.

Additional copies of *WATCH YOUR WALK*
and other Victor Classics titles
are available from your local Christian bookseller.

If you have enjoyed this book,
or if it has had an impact on your life,
we would like to hear from you.

Please contact us at:

VICTOR BOOKS
Cook Communications Ministries, Dept. 201
4050 Lee Vance View
Colorado Springs, CO 80918

Or visit our Web site:
www.cookministries.com

Victor®
The Bible Teacher's Teacher